# DESIGNER HOME
# SEWING

QUARRY

GLOUCESTER MASSACHUSETTS

# DESIGNER HOME SEWING

QUARRY BOOKS

Step-by-Step Instructions for 30 Easy-to-Make Projects

LINDA LEE

First published in the United States of America by
Quarry Books, a member of
Quayside Publishing Group
33 Commercial Street
Gloucester, Massachusetts  01930-5089
Telephone: (978) 282-9590
Fax: (978) 283-2742
www.rockpub.com

**Library of Congress Cataloging-in-Publication Data**
Lee, Linda, [date]
   Designer home sewing : step-by-step instructions for 30 easy-to-make projects / Linda Lee.
        p.   cm.
   Includes index.
   ISBN 1-59253-206-3 (pbk.)
   1.  Household linens. 2.  Textile fabrics in interior decoration. 3.  Machine sewing.  I. Title.
   TT387.L43 2005
   646.2'1—dc22                                    2005018395
                                                   CIP


ISBN 1-59253-206-3

10 9 8 7 6 5 4 3 2 1

Design: Laura McFadden Design Inc.
Cover images: Courtesy of Arthur Sanderson & Sons/
        www.sanderson-uk.com
Illustrations by: Lainé Roundy

Printed in Singapore

# contents

# Introduction

It's all about the fabric! The simplest room can be transformed with the addition of fabric—sometimes a little, maybe a lot. One of the pleasures of sewing is knowing that you can gather some fabric and make something wonderful for your home. After years of sewing garments and other things for myself, I signed up for a Quilt-in-a-Night class. At eight o'clock in the morning, after a long night at the sewing machine, I arrived home with a completed quilt top. My husband was so impressed that even today, years later, he drags that quilt out and places it on our bed—it's his favorite. That's when I realized that giving the gift of your sewing talents to someone who you care about is very special.

There are other reasons to consider sewing for your home. It is rare when we can start from scratch to decorate a room. It's usually necessary to work with something that exists in a room—a quilt, an heirloom chair, a good rug. Maybe it's not your favorite thing, but it's important to keep and too expensive to replace. But trends in home decorating are just like the ever-changing trends in fashion; there are certain color schemes that are in vogue at any given time, but upholstered furniture, curtains, and other commercially available accessories may not be available in the colors you need to coordinate with what you have. It is much easier to find the right fabric to change your room than to find a finished product in just the right size and price.

A RICH ARRAY OF FABRICS DIFFERING IN DESIGN, BUT UNITED BY SHARED COLORS AND HUES GIVE A ROOM A LIVELY, YET UNIFIED LOOK. FABRIC ACCESSORIES WITH WARM, EARTHY COLORS LIKE THESE, IN TERRA-COTTA AND SAND, BRING A SUNNY GLOW TO A ROOM THAT IS SHORT ON NATURAL LIGHT OR HAS NEUTRAL WALL COLOR.

If you have ever hired a professional workroom to make a few items for your home, you know how expensive it can be. This is when sewing things yourself can really be a money-saver. Fabrics and trims for interiors are much more readily available to the home sewer today and the prices range from the best of bargains to very high-end. But now, by sewing your own soft furnishings, you save the labor cost, which can be as expensive or more than the cost of the materials.

Perhaps the most valuable reason to sew furnishings and accessories for your own home is to bring your own stamp into your interior, to personalize and make your surroundings feel like you want to spend time there. It is always a good idea to hire a professional interior designer to coordinate ideas to achieve the right look, but ultimately, it's your choice and you want it to be right for you and your family for a long time.

This book nudges you in the right direction, helping you make good decisions when selecting fabrications that express your style, giving you great tips for sifting through the myriad products available and achieving just what works. You will find sources for inspiration and you will get permission to break a few rules when putting it all together. Plus there are thirty projects that include great techniques that you can apply to any number of sewing projects, not just the ones in the book. Change the fabric, add a detail, alter the size, but most of all, get that sewing machine out of the closet and get ready to change your interior and your life. Have fun!

# CHAPTER ONE

# Designing for Yourself

COLLECTING IS A KEY WORD to use when organizing your thoughts about how you want to decorate a room. This doesn't mean that you have to collect "things." What it does mean is that before you begin to decorate, you need to collect and record your thoughts about what pleases you, inspires you, and makes you and your family operate effectively in your surroundings.

## INSPIRATION

One of the most important, and helpful, exercises that I have used for a number of years is to keep notebooks of inspiration—images (photographs, pages torn from magazines, and other sources) that remind me of an experience, a time, or a place or that just plain intrigues me for reasons that I don't always understand or even try to understand. They are scrapbooks, of sorts, except that they are not particularly organized, they are not finely presented, and they are added to routinely.

### Journals and Notebooks

I slip the images into clear plastic sleeves and add them to ring-binder notebooks of similar images. The notebooks are organized by a general topic, such as pillows, window shades, table accessories, and bed covers, and labeled accordingly.

After years of collecting these images, it's amazing how I have found that I have a penchant for collecting similar ideas. While color schemes may change, and the level of sophistication of magazine journalism has improved, and the images may be more beautiful, the elements themselves are amazingly similar.

### Magazine, Graphic Art, and Book

I subscribe to almost every kind of interior decorating magazine, from those that showcase the most elegant and unattainable interiors to those that show the most basic and mainstream rooms. I no longer keep the magazines for very long—storing them became a problem. Now I immediately flip through and tear out any number of pages that appeal to me. It's an immediate impulse, no great thought is given to why I'm tearing a page out. I might be attracted to a paint color, a pillow detail, a window treatment, or simply the overall mood of the room.

The graphics and advertising industry is another rich source of design influence for interior decorators. I collect postcards, invitations, brochures, and other printed matter, adding them to my binders. Graphic artists are just as tuned in to what's new and happening in terms of colors, shapes, and spatial treatments as fashion designers and interior designers.

My library of books is also a really important part of my inspiration collections. There's nothing better than a trip to the local bookstore for an hour or two of browsing the interiors and architectural sections as well as the crafts and photography stacks. A book may sit on my shelf for a long time. But the day will come when I pick it up, flip through a few pages, and something on the page will send me in a new direction—and I'll feel inspired. The image may not have even been close to what I thought I was looking for, but it triggered a memory or something on an unconscious level, and I'm on my way.

Stacks of fabrics, just sitting there waiting to inspire you, are all part of the germinating process in determining your style and what makes you feel good. Buy small yardages of fabrics that strike your fancy to have on hand when the mood to be creative slips up on you.

Fashions from the '50s and '60s, both in furniture styles and colorations, have enjoyed a resurgence in popularity. Bold stylized prints and strong contrasting colors appeal to a younger generation and the always young-at-heart.

## Fashion Forecast

Fashion designers are always on the leading edge of trends and lifestyles, and I add pages from fashion magazines regularly to my idea binders. By reading fashion magazines and studying the clothes in the stores and on the runways, you can get a real feel for what's new in color schemes and general mood. Comparisons between fashions and interiors are inevitable. While garment fashions may change more dramatically and more often, there is no question that interior styles follow that lead and move along in a more fashionable way than ever before. For example, a retro fabric used in a handbag may show up later as a rug design—sometimes they are even designed by the same person. Fashion designers who have their own clothing lines may also design for furniture makers, dinnerware companies, and bed linen companies. You can easily emulate professional trend experts who watch all disciplines to predict what we will want to wear and how we will decorate our living spaces.

## Design Notions

Having a stash of fabrics, ribbons, buttons, and trims is an essential part of starting the creative process. I have ceased buying fabric for specific projects. I simply buy a yard or two of what strikes me when I come across it. When I'm stuck (designer's block), I'll get a group of fabrics out of the cabinets, spread them out on the floor, and visually soak them in. I might leave them there for a few days, walking around them, over them, and on them, letting them filter through my psyche. While a yard or two may not make more than a pillow or a few placemats, at least I have something to work with, such as color, pattern, and texture combinations, which may lead to larger projects.

## Travel Influences

Not everyone has the luxury of traveling the world. But opening your eyes to the geography near you and its influences is a very exciting experience. If you are traveling, absorb the shapes, textures, light, color, and patterns that you see everywhere. It might be the muted adobe colors of Albuquerque's Old Town, the view of San Francisco's white skyline from the Golden Gate Bridge, the color of redbud trees blooming in Kansas, or the neighborhood murals painted on the playground walls in New York City. Even looking through travel magazines and cooking magazines featuring recipes from exotic locales can give you a sensory experience from which to draw inspiration.

THIS HANDSOME COLLECTION OF VINTAGE RIBBONS AND FABRIC SAMPLES IS JUST A SMALL SAMPLING OF THE MYRAID CHOICES AVAILABLE TODAY.

# EXPRESSING YOUR STYLE

It all begins by asking yourself some questions and, making some notes. The way you live; the things you love; and the kinds of colors, textures, and styles that naturally appeal to you are important to evaluate and try to put into place when you set out to decorate a room—or several rooms.

### Evaluating Your Lifestyle

Decorating is a very personal art form, and you'll need to investigate your lifestyle wants and needs in order to fulfill them. Do you like to entertain small groups in an intimate setting or throw big parties with people all over the house? Do you have pets that have furniture privileges? Do you need to see sunlight filtering through your rooms, or do you feel safer in a dark, quiet spot? Do you own family heirlooms that you love and want to display and use, or are you drawn to the sleek and simple lines of post-modern furniture? By answering a few questions—and there are no right or wrong answers—you can begin to explore your lifestyle and design preferences.

### Assessing Your Belongings

Take an actual inventory of what items are important to you that you need to keep in a room. Few of us are able or willing to start over by buying all new furniture and fabrics on a whim. Sentiment and family pressure are bound to influence how you feel about particular furnishings. Photograph pieces of your furniture and stand back and really study them with a new eye. Perhaps they are not how you remember them. Is a piece worthy of a new slipcover? Would the addition of a pillow or two or a new throw give it a new look without altering the essence of the piece?

### Recording Your Feelings

By collecting photographs and visual materials as described earlier, similarities in images will emerge, and you will begin to understand some of the nuances of your personal style preferences. Record your feelings about whether you like cool colors or warm colors, neutrals or high contrasting colors. Decide whether you prefer busy patterns, mixtures of patterns, geometric patterns, or very little pattern. Evaluate whether you like smooth fabrics or textural surfaces.

THIS ROOM IS BUILT AROUND A THEME OF OLD TOYS AND
TEDDY BEARS. THE NATURAL MATERIALS AND COLORS ALLOW
THE COLLECTABLES TO STAND OUT AND DOMINATE THE LOOK.

JOURNALS WITH SAMPLES OF FABRICS AND TRIMS PROVIDE A HANDY WAY TO KEEP GOOD RECORDS OF COLOR AND MATERIAL SELECTIONS AND ARE PORTABLE WHEN SELECTING PAINT COLORS, FLOOR MATERIALS, AND ACCESSORIES.

## Making a Design Board

Keep a journal with bits of materials stapled or taped to your pages of notes, throw scraps of fabrics and colors into clear envelope file folders, or make a design board. If you are planning to change a number of things in a room, then a sample board is quite useful for collecting your thoughts, and it is portable enough to take along as you shop. This visual demonstration of all the fabrics, paint colors, and other finishes will give you an idea of the overall effect you want to achieve and will save you money in the long run by preventing a few mistakes. As you collect your samples, try to find pieces that are in proportion to how they will appear in the room. For example, the paint sample should be large, a fabric sample for the sofa should be smaller than the paint sample, but larger than the fabric for the adjacent chair and the accent pillow or trim. Fold or bunch fabric that will be draped or gathered as opposed to fabrics that will be stretched flat on a piece of furniture. Tape and glue the samples to a piece of foam core board or pin them to a bulletin board or slip them behind strips of ribbon or elastic on a board. Stand back, squint, and see what stands out and doesn't fit in. Keep working at it until everything feels right.

# COLOR SENSE

For most people, choosing colors is the hardest part of decorating a room. Whether it's a paint color or a fabric decision, it's a commitment and it can be intimidating. Making the wrong decision is frustrating, time-consuming, and expensive to change. The fear factor makes some people freeze, resulting in rooms that have no character or become a hodgepodge of ideas.

## The Power of Color

Color is the most powerful design element in a room and is very possibly the singular thing that people remember about a space. Back in the days when I was selling furniture from maker's catalogs, I would show a client a few photos of similar chairs, with some photos in black and white and some photos shown in color. Inevitably the client would choose the furniture style in the color photograph, even though it might have been exactly the same chair as the black and white one and cost more money. This is when I realized the degree to which color influences us.

Color can make spaces seem larger: visually extend walls, raise ceilings, and eliminate corners. High contrast colors in saturated tones are so all-absorbing to the eye that cracks, blemishes, and awkward room details are masked. Rich fabrics in deep color tones make an impact on their own. The eye is drawn to the color first, then the shape and placement later. By contrast, neutral, pale tones highlight the architectural details of a room. You are more aware of the spaces, and the relationships of elements, furniture, and decorative details to one another. But ultimately, it is your own personal preferences in color that matter. If you find that you are drawn to a particular hue or shade of color, then by all means try to use it in your decorating.

The effects of color on walls, floors, or fabrics are influenced by the texture of the material surfaces, how they are combined with nearby colors, and whether they are viewed under natural light or artificial light—and more specifically—fluorescent or incandescent artificial light. When selecting colors, whether paint colors or fabric colors, it is important to look at the largest samples available in the setting in which they will be used and to see all of them together at one time.

## Color Palettes

Color schemes come in two basic categories. Cool, or receding, tones include blue, blue-green, green, blue-lilac and some grays. Cool colors calm a room and make the room appear larger. But they can also make a room appear too cold, so they need to be in a space that is already warmed by sunlight or where there is a lot of activity. Warm colors appear to advance, or come forward toward you. Colors, such as red, pink, orange, apricot, peach, yellow, terra cotta, and tan enclose an area and invite you into it. But sometimes these appear too confining, and so need to be limited to the paler values, such as pink or apricot rather than red or orange, in small rooms. The warmth of the color palette makes this space comfortable and inviting.

Neutral color schemes derive from natural materials, such as wood, cane, marble, brick, stone, linen, and undyed cotton. They can be cool or warm and used in a very restrained way. But they often act as the background for accents and artwork. One of the challenges in working with a neutral scheme is to have a variety of textures and tonal contrasts.

Bold colors and patterns are like warm tones because they appear to come toward you and will dominate a room. They will make a large area cozier and create a busy atmosphere. Small-scale patterns are like cool colors—they appear to recede. They help make a small space seem larger, but they can be somewhat bland if not used in an interesting color scheme.

THIS GROUP OF MATERIALS IS A BEAUTIFUL BLEND OF FABRICS IN SIMILAR COLOR TONES, BUT THE MIX OF TEXTURES IS CLASSY AND INTERESTING—FABRICS WITH SHEEN, TONE-ON-TONE PATTERNS, SHEER FABRICS, AND UPHOLSTERY-WEIGHT TEXTURES. EVEN THE TRIMS ADD TEXTURE.

SATURATED TONES ARE USED IN SHARP CONTRASTS TO BRIGHTEN AND ENLIVEN A ROOM. THE JEWEL-LIKE BRILLIANCE OF THESE COLORS MAKES A ROOM WELCOMING AND INTIMATE.

If you are not drawn to any particular color scheme, look to nature as a good source for a color palette. It is very common to describe colors in terms of nature–colors such as moss green, buttercup yellow, cherry red, midnight blue. These associations with nature on a grand scale, as in the changing colors of the landscape, or the colors of nature close at hand, such as in a garden, are inherently pleasant and are easy to emulate.

An easy starting point for a color scheme is to select a patterned fabric with many colors, an upholstery fabric, or a large-scaled drapery fabric. Echo the various colors on the other surfaces in the room, plucking out your favorites. It may well be that you never use the original piece of fabric, but its purpose was served.

Beware of trying to match colors to photographs in magazines and books. Lighting, photography, and printing all affect how colors look on slick pages and it is almost impossible to get the exact color. While publications are certainly great sources of inspirations for color schemes, there are too many variables in your own setting and you can easily be disappointed.

COLORS FROM NATURE ARE OFTEN TAKEN FOR GRANTED, BUT THE MOST PERFECT COLOR COMBINATIONS ARE RIGHT BEFORE OUR EYES IN THE FLOWER COLORS MIXED WITH GREENS AND FRUITS AND VEGETABLES JUST PICKED FORM THE GARDEN.

NEARLY ALL THE COLORS FOUND IN THE LARGE-SCALE PRINT ARE
DRAWN INTO THE SETTING AGAIN, FROM THE PAINT COLOR TO THE
ACCENT COLOR. THE SCALE OF THE COORDINATING FABRICS IS
VARIED AND WORKS WELL IN THE OVERALL SCHEME.

SHRIMP AND BUTTERCREAM, WHICH ARE
VARIATIONS OF ORANGE AND YELLOW, ARE
COLORS CLOSE TO ONE ANOTHER ON THE
COLOR WHEEL, BUT HERE THEY ARE
INTENSE AND SATURATED. THE SECRET TO
COMBINING THESE TWO COLORS IS TO MAKE
SURE THEY ARE SIMILAR IN VALUE.

## FINDING THE FABRICS

Fabric gives a room its character. It can totally alter it, and it certainly enhances it. Choosing it is the fun part.

### Solid Colors

Solid colors rarely go out of style. It may seem easy to select a group of solid colors but, in fact, it is relatively difficult. One way to use solid colors is to mix shades and tones such as combining a medium sea blue with an aqua and a lighter sky blue. But contrasting colors in the same value or visual weight, such as a strong red-orange and a deep blue, are also effective. The same color can look different in various fabrics when each is a different texture ranging from smooth and shiny to pebbly and matte. If the colors are strong, you can get away with subtle or smooth textures. You will need richer textures and interesting weaves when using neutrals and refined colors. Some of the most beautiful solid fabrics with wonderful textures are wool and velvet. Combine these with the smooth textures of satin and damask, and you have pure luxury.

## Checks, Stripes, and Plaids

Checks, stripes, and plaids are very traditional, but in recent times, they have been recolored and rescaled and are now definitely on the scene. Stripes range from glorious Regency satins to casual French ticking. Cotton and linen checks are plentiful, but when lined and backed, and used in heavyweight draperies and upholstery, they suit interiors ranging from the country cottage to the modernist loft. Plaids are traditionally considered country, but silk plaids in large-scale, bold color combinations are very contemporary additions to monochromatic rooms.

## Florals

Historical document fabrics are still used to reproduce today's floral fabric designs. The new florals differ from the originals in their scale and coloring. Bright flowers are printed on fresh white or figured backgrounds. Tiny, antique prints found as drawer liners are boldly oversized and punched with serious colors. Florals are now being combined with animal prints rather than the standard plaids. And many new fabrics have been laundered or sandwashed to soften them and make them appear old. If you're working with a design board (see page 20), cover the board with the floral fabric and add to it the trims, the wallpaper, the paint color, and other interesting fabrics that you think will produce the effect you are trying to achieve in a room remodel.

A CRISP AWNING STRIPE FABRIC USED IN THESE STRAIGHTFORWARD DRAPERY TREATMENTS ACCENTUATES THE ULTRA-TALL RECESSED WINDOWS OF AN INDOOR/OUTDOOR SPACE.

THIS FREE-SPIRITED MIX OF COMPLEMENTARY FLORALS COMBINES NICELY WITH COTTON SEERSUCKER AND TICKING STRIPES FOR A CASUAL COTTAGE-STYLE LOOK.

## The Classics

Silks and damasks, pictorials and toiles are considered the classics. All these fabrics are the aristocratic grand masters of the interior world. Silks and damasks are rich and expensive but have never gone out of style. Even though silk fades in the sunlight, designers are using them for window treatments, but interlining them with hefty flannel and lining them with good sun-resistant materials. Use the expensive damasks in small quantities—such as patchworked into pillows. Pictorial designs are extremely old, but manufacturers have revamped them into scaled patterns that work in modern interiors with interesting backgrounds in today's color schemes. They are fun and fashionable.

PICTORIALS AND TOILES, BOTH FRENCH AND ENGLISH, HAVE BEEN AROUND FOR CENTURIES, BUT THEY ARE JUST AS POPULAR TODAY AS EVER. USED BOTH IN FORMAL AND CASUAL SETTINGS, THEY ARE VERSATILE AND EASY TO LIVE WITH.

## Where to Shop

Not too long ago, if you wanted to buy a few yards of good quality decorator fabric, you'd consult an interior designer. While that is certainly and always a wonderful option, interior-design fabrics are now more easily available to the average consumer, interested in making her own soft furnishings.

There are specialty shops in most large communities that sell fabrics off the bolt by the yard, with most of them displayed in coordinated color groupings. Along with the fabrics, you can buy the pillow forms, the drapery rods and hardware, the cordings and trims, order custom-made furniture, and get personal help from on-site decorators. Discount fabric and craft stores also sell the fabrics, but the design consultation is not on hand at these lower-end stores.

Antique shops are a good source for vintage linens, such as old stripes and checks, and fragments of other potentially usable fabrics. Perusing flea markets and yard sales may produce some surprising finds in linens and fabrics that can be restyled into new products.

Online sources have exploded in recent times. Without being able to touch the fabric, it is always a good idea to order the minimum quantity as a test. If you do a little research on fabric types and names, it is easier to know what you are ordering before making an expensive online purchase.

## THE ART OF FINISHING

After selecting fabrics and colors and deciding where and how they will be used, it is tempting to think that you are done. But the fun has just begun. Now it's time to think about the decorative touches and the unique details that make the room sing.

Finishing touches are generally thought of as accessory pieces, such as pillows, drapery tiebacks, or lamps. But it is just as important to consider how each piece of furniture; every window covering, and all the accessories are edged, finished, trimmed, and detailed. Should the pillow have trim and how is it to be used? Are the tiebacks made in the same fabric as the draperies or are they a special shape and material? Are the lamp bases decorative enough or should the shades be edged with tassels or fringe?

There is nothing wrong with leaving everything in a room completely unadorned. In fact, some of the most beautiful interiors are those without a single accessory. The finishes and materials are strong enough on their own to carry the room. But it takes a special eye to work with pure line, shape, color, and texture without adding flourishes. More often, rooms feel more complete and more comfortable when there is special attention given to every detail, particularly when working with fabrics.

Window coverings are primary features in a room. Even though a sofa may be the largest element in a room, it's the draperies that catch your eye and are usually what people comment on when first walking into a space. Not only are the draperies, curtains, and shades important, but how they are detailed emphasizes the design of the window treatment. The detail may be as simple as an applied band of contrasting fabric—perhaps the same fabric also used in a pillow—or as showy as a fluted and gilt drapery rod and finials. The details do not need to be fussy or fancy, but they do need to accentuate the line of the drapery and work with other decorative elements in a room, perhaps even repeating a fabric or color that is used elsewhere.

There has been an explosion in the production of decorative trimmings—tassels in every size and coloration with coordinating rosettes, twisted cordings, and bullion fringes, intricately woven gimp cords, flat braids and embroidered braids, flanged trims with tassels, beads and pearls, feathers, and lace. The possibilities are endless and it's fun to think about how to use them. These are what will set your room apart from the ordinary. Use a tassel and rosette at the corner of a sofa cushion for a new twist on an old standard. Sew a tassel trim to the surface of the edge of a pillow allowing the flange to show instead of inserting it into an edge as is more commonly done. Sew glass beaded trim to the edge of a drapery, giving it a subtle, glistening definition.

A STRIPED FABRIC FACING IS SEWN TO THE INSIDE OF THIS DRAPERY. SOFTLY FOLDING THE FACING TO THE OUTSIDE ACCENTUATES THE DRAPERY TOP.

A TASSEL AND ROSETTE FINISH THE CORNER OF THIS TRADITIONAL SOFA. REPEATING THE ROSETTES AND ADDING BULLION FRINGE HELP SET THIS SOFA APART FROM THE ORDINARY.

SOMETIMES THE BEST PART OF A TASSEL TRIM IS THE WOVEN FLANGE. SEW IT TO THE TOP OF THE PILLOW FOR A SPECIAL ACCENT.

A TWO-COLOR COTTON FRINGE ADDED TO THE BOTTOM OF THIS LAMPSHADE REINTRODUCES THE COLORS FROM THE TABLE SKIRT.

CLEAR ACRYLIC BEADS ADD SPARKLE TO AN OTHERWISE PLAIN DRAPERY.

NATURAL SHELL AND BEADED TRIM ADDS JUST THE RIGHT EDGING TO THIS TROPICAL FLORAL THROW.

TWO EMBELLISHMENT TECHNIQUES— APPLIQUÉ AND EMBROIDERY—ARE COMBINED TO CREATE THIS CHARMING CHICKEN MOTIF ON A WICKER CHAIR PILLOW.

With the advent of new technologies in home sewing machines, embellishing the surfaces of fabrics is now amazingly easy. By changing a few presser feet and stitch selections on your sewing machine, you can create interesting effects unlike anything you can buy in a store. Practically any design from a simple graphic to a multicolored dimensional design can be adapted for use as a fabric appliqué. Contrasting motifs can be appliquéd to a fabric using a satin stitch or a blanket stitch in rayon or polyester decorative threads.

Machine embroidery is one of the newest and largest trends in sewing. With thousands of embroidery designs available through sewing machine dealerships and on the Internet, plus the ability of modern sewing machines to digitize a design and reproduce it in thread, opens up the possibility of really customizing your accessories and furnishings. Add in the hundreds of thread colors and types on the market today, and machine embroidery is now a serious option for the home sewer.

The scope of decorative details is as great as your imagination allows, from strong modern effects to classically elegant statements. Study the immense resources of magazines and books and research historically significant interiors. Adding the flourish is as old of a concept as decorating itself. The potential for creativity is everywhere.

A WHITE PILLOW NOW MAKES A STATEMENT IN THE ROOM WHEN BLACK APPLIQUÉS ARE SEWN TO THE FACE OF THIS PILLOW.

# CHAPTER TWO

# Projects

→ The Illustrated steps for the following projects are keyed to indicate the wrong side of the fabric **(WS)** and the right side of the fabric **(RS)** for your reference.

# Stagecoach **Roller Shade**

THOUGH FLAT WHEN UNFURLED, this shade is much like a Roman shade, except it lacks the rings and cording. Fabric straps that tie under the bottom roller set the shade to the desired length, to determine the amount of view through the window and add a decorative detail.decorative detail.

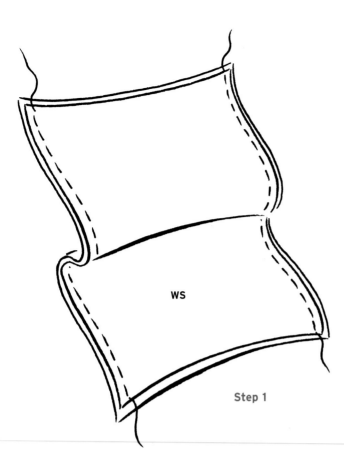

WS

WS

Step 1

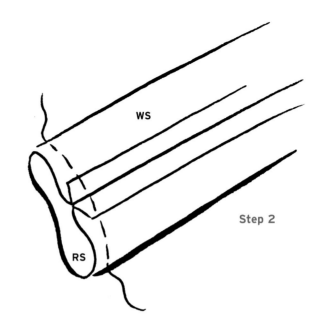

WS

RS

Step 2

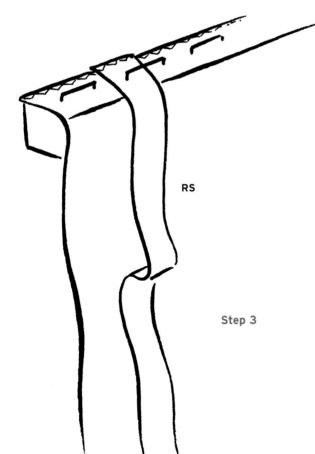

RS

Step 3

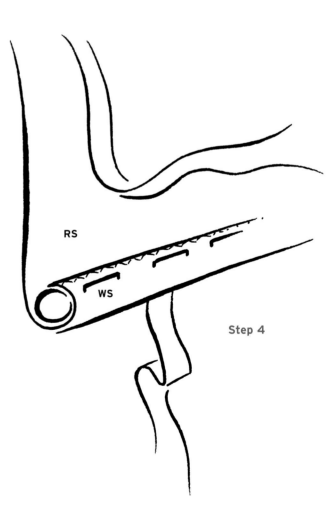

RS

WS

Step 4

## MATERIALS

**Note:** *The items in this list are for one Stagecoach Roller Shade.*

- *Fabric for the shade*
- *Contrasting fabric for the straps*
- *1¼" (3.2 cm) diameter wood dowel rod for the bottom roller*
- *1" X 1" (2.5 X 2.5 cm) wood mounting board*
- *2 small L-brackets*
- *Staple gun*

## PROJECT TECHNIQUES

- *Length Addition for Repeats (page 148)*
- *Seam Positions for Fabric Widths (page 148)*

## Preparation

Measure the inside width and height of the window. Subtract ½" (1.2 cm) from the finished width and add ½" (1.2 cm) seam allowances to all the sides. Add a total of 12" (30.5 cm) to the height, for wrapping the top wood mounting board and the bottom roller.

Cut two panels of fabric, both matching the total width and height measurements. If the window is wider than the fabric, add additional panels by making vertical seams where the straps will be positioned.

Cut four straps, each 5" (12.7 cm)-wide, and as long as the height of the window plus 16" (40.6 cm).

Cut the 1" X 1" (2.5 X 2.5 cm) wood mounting board ½" (1.2 cm) less than the finished width of the panel.

## Construction

**Step 1** With right sides together, sew the two panels together along each side. Turn the shade to the outside. With the raw upper edges held together, finish the edge.

**Step 2** Fold a strap in half lengthwise with right sides together and sew the long seam. At one short end, press the seam allowances open and center the seam on the strap. Sew across the end. Turn the strap to the outside and press it, keeping the seam centered along the entire length of the underside. With the raw upper edges held together, finish the edge. Repeat to make the remaining straps.

**Step 3** Divide the width of the shade into fourths. Placing one strap on the right side of the shade and one strap on the wrong side of the shade, pin the straps to the top of the shade. Repeat to attach the remaining straps.

**Step 4** Cover the wood mounting board with the shade fabric, or paint the wood mounting board to complement the shade fabric. Position the shade, right side up, over the top of the board and allow the shade to hang over the front of the board. Staple the top of the shade and straps to the board.

**Step 5** Cut the bottom roller ½" (1.2 cm) less than the finished width of the shade. Cover the ends neatly with the shade fabric. Staple the bottom raw edge of the shade to the dowel so that the dowel will roll to the front of the shade. Leave the straps hanging loosely.

**Step 6** Roll the bottom dowel a few times and hold it in place with the tied straps. Adjust the desired length, as necessary.

**Step 7** Using the L-brackets, install the shade inside the window frame.

# Swagged Roman Shade

A CUTWORK LINEN PANEL, either new or vintage, is the perfect starting material for a swagged Roman shade. This project is a loose variation on the traditional Roman shade, except that it has fewer drawstrings.

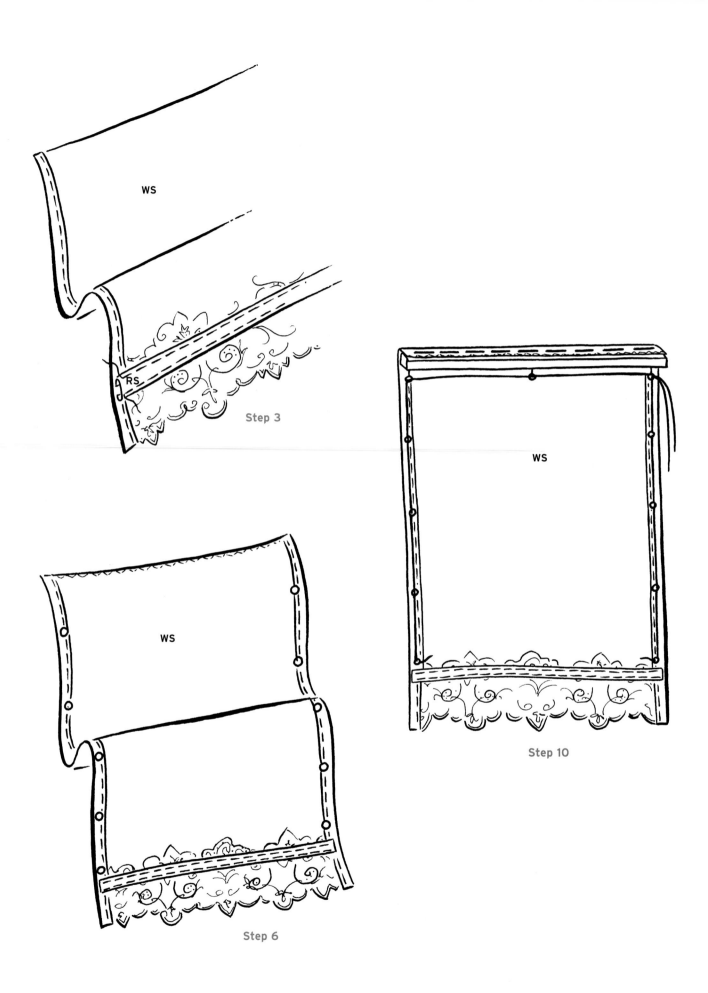

WS

RS

**Step 3**

WS

**Step 6**

WS

**Step 10**

## MATERIALS

**Note:** *The items in this list are for one Swagged Roman Shade.*

- *Cutwork linen panel for the shade*
- *Matching solid-color fabric for the rod*
- *Pocket and mounting board cover*
- *Polyester thread*
- *Shade cord*
- *1" X 2" (2.5 X 5.1 cm) wood mounting board*
- *2 screw eyes*
- *2 small L-brackets*
- *Cleat*
- *Hand sewing needle*
- *Shade pull*
- *Shade rings*
- *Staple gun*
- *Wood screen door molding*

## PROJECT TECHNIQUES

- *Double-Fold Hem (page 141)*
- *Edgestitch (page 141)*
- *Finish (page 141)*
- *Topstitch (page 141)*

## Preparation

Measure the inside width and height of the window. Subtract ½" (1.2 cm) from the finished width. For the total width, add 4" (10 cm) for two side hems. For the total length, add 2" (5.1 cm) to the top. Add 4" (10 cm) to the bottom hem if not using a finished cutwork edge.

Cut a piece of solid-color fabric 2" (5.1 cm) X the finished width of the shade plus 1" (2.5 cm) for the rod pocket.

Cut a piece of solid-color fabric large enough to cover all sides and both ends of the mounting board.

Cut a piece of screen door molding the width of the inside window less 1" (2.5 cm).

## Construction

**Step 1** If not using a finished cutwork bottom edge, make a 2" (5.1 cm)-wide double-fold hem at the bottom.

**Step 2** Make 1" (2.5 cm) double-fold hems at both sides of the panel.

**Step 3** Press ½" (1.2 cm) to the wrong side on all edges of the solid-color fabric strip. To make a rod pocket, pin the strip a few inches above the bottom of the cutwork bottom edge, with wrong sides together. Edgestitch along the top and bottom edges of the strip, leaving the short ends open.

**Step 4** Finish the top edge of the shade.

**Step 5** Mark the ring locations along each side hem. To find the vertical space between rings, measure the distance from the top of the finished shade to the rod pocket and divide this number by 8" (20.3 cm). Round off to the nearest whole number to get the number of spaces. Divide the same distance by the number of spaces to arrive at the exact space size.

**Step 6** Using doubled polyester thread, hand sew the rings to the side hems on the wrong side of the shade.

**Step 7** Wrap the mounting board, covering all the sides and both ends. Position the shade, right side up, over the covered mounting board and staple the shade to the 2" (5.1 cm)-wide top of the board.

**Step 8** Insert screw eyes on the underside of the mounting board, directly above each column of rings and one in the center of the board.

**Step 9** Cut two lengths of shade cord long enough to go through a column of rings, across the top of the shade to the right and halfway down the side.

**Step 10** With the shade wrong side up, tie one end of the cord to the bottom right ring and thread the cord up through all the rings in the column. Pass the cord from left to right through the screw eye at the top and let the remainder of the cord hang down the right side. Tie the other cord to the bottom left ring and thread the cord up through all the rings in the column, and then through the left, center, and right screw eyes. Let the remainder of the cord hang down the right side.

**Step 11** Cover both ends of the screen door molding with solid-color fabric. Insert the screen door molding into the bottom casing. With the shade unfurled, adjust the tension of the cords so the shade draws up in even horizontal folds when the cords are pulled. Lower the shade and knot the cords together just below the screw eye. Pull the cords through a shade pull, knot, and trim the ends. Slide the pull over the knot.

**Step 12** Install the shade and mount a cleat on the window frame to secure the cords.

# Layered Panels

WHAT LOOKS LIKE A SERIES of separate fabrics is simply one folded panel. Layering creates the illusion of color changes in the fabric. The semi-sheer fabric gives a sense of privacy while allowing filtered light into the space.

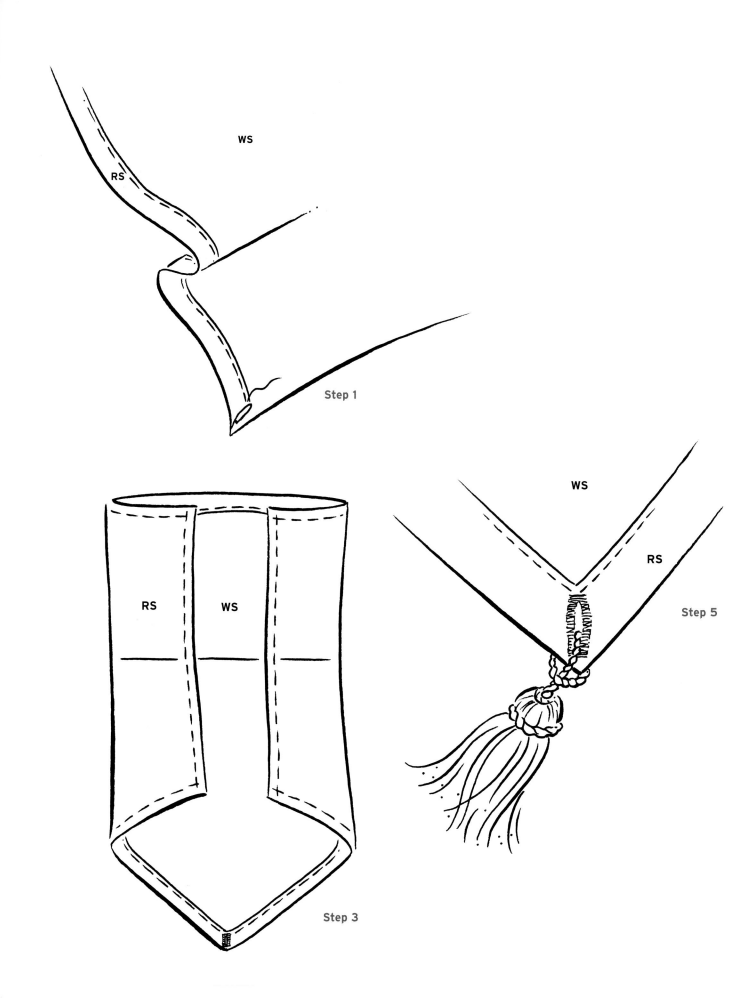

WS

RS

Step 1

RS

WS

Step 3

WS

RS

Step 5

## MATERIALS

**Note:** *The items in this list are for one Layered Panel.*

• *Gauzelike fabric*
• *Pattern paper*
• *Tassel*
• *Wood curtain rod and brackets*

## PROJECT TECHNIQUES

• *Double-Fold Hem (page 141)*
• *Topstitch (page 141)*

## Construction

**Step 1** Make ½" (1.2 cm)-wide double-fold hems on all sides, in the following order: the sides, the bottom diagonal edges, and the top.

**Step 2** Make a small machine-sewn buttonhole in the hem allowance at the bottom center point.

**Step 3** Fold the panel along the side fold-lines to the wrong side.

**Step 4** Fold the panel along the horizontal foldline and drape over a wooden rod.

**Step 5** Loop the tassel cord through the buttonhole to hang the tassel.

## Preparation

Measure the inside height and width of the window. Divide the window width in fourths. Add one-fourth to the panel width twice, for the side folds. Add 2" (5.1 cm) total for side hem allowances.

Make a paper pattern to the dimensions determined.

Find the center of the width for the bottom point. Draw diagonal lines radiating from the center point for the bottom angle.

Determine the length of the face from the bottom point to the top of the rod and add the length of the desired back drop (the fabric that drapes over the curtain rod and hangs down the back). Add a 1" (2.5 cm) hem allowance to the top and another 1" (2.5 cm) to the bottom. To the paper pattern, draw a horizontal line across the panel to make a fold line for the back drop. Draw vertical fold lines to mark the outermost fourths.

## Tip

A DECORATIVE DETAIL PLACED ON THE CENTER PANEL IS A NICE FINISHING TOUCH. HERE ARE SOME IDEAS.
1. PRINT IMAGES ON PHOTO TRANSFER PAPER AND IRON THE TRANSFER ONTO THE FABRIC.
2. STENCIL IMAGES ONTO THE FABRIC USING FABRIC PAINT.
3. HAND- OR MACHINE-EMBROIDER MOTIFS IN A PLEASING DESIGN ONTO THE FABRIC.

# Bandanna Valance

BUTTONS, FRINGE, AND PIPING trim these scarf like valances. If sewing buttons onto fabric seems too daunting, buy a whimsical fabric and edge the valance with a fun fringed trim.

## MATERIALS

Note: *The items in this list are for one Bandanna Valance.*

- *Fabric for valance front*
- *Contrasting fabric for covered cording*
- *Lining fabric for valance back*
- *Cotton cording*
- *Fringe*
- *1" X 2" (2.5 X 5.1 cm) wood mounting board*
- *2 small L-brackets*
- *Miscellaneous buttons*
- *Pattern paper*
- *Staple gun*

## PROJECT TECHNIQUES

- *Making Covered Piping (page 145)*
- *Buttons (page 140)*
- *Finish (page 141)*

### Preparation

Measure the inside width of the window.

Measure the desired finished length of the valance at the (shorter) sides.

Measure the desired length of the valance at the (longer) center.

Use the measurements to draw the shape of the finished valance on the pattern paper.

Add 2" (5.1 cm) at the top and ½" (1.2 cm) seam allowances on all the other sides.

Using the paper pattern, cut one fabric piece and one lining piece.

Cut the mounting board ½" (1.2 cm) less than the finished width of the valance.

Cover the sides and ends of the mounting board with lining fabric and staple it in place.

### Construction

**Step 1** Make enough covered cording to cover the sides and bottom of the valance. Remove the filler cord in the last 2" (5.1 cm) of each end of the covered cord.

**Step 2** Sew the covered cording to the right side of the sides and bottom of the valance.

**Step 3** Sew miscellaneous buttons to the right side of the valance, if desired. Sew to within 2" (5.1 cm) of the top.

**Step 4** Sew the fringe trim to the right side of the valance, sandwiching the covered cording between the fabric and the fringe.

**Step 5** With right sides together, sew the lining to the fabric along the sides and the bottom, leaving the top edge open. Turn the valance to the outside.

**Step 6** Randomly sew buttons to the fringe ends.

**Step 7** With the top edges held together, finish the raw edges. Staple the top edge of the valance to the top of the mounting board. See step 4 of Stagecoach Roller Shade on page 37.

**Step 8** Install the valance in inside of the window using the L-brackets.

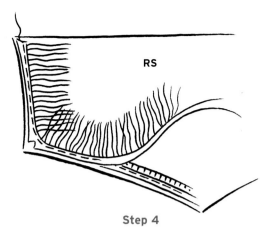

Step 4

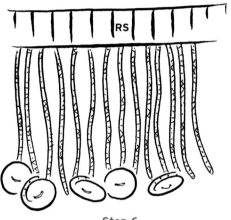

Step 6

# Sheer Room Divider

USE A SINGLE WIDTH OF SHEER FABRIC such as gauze to mini-
mally separate two spaces. While defining an area, it softens the
mood of a room and allows light to filter through, and it is easily
moved when necessary.

## MATERIALS

- *Sheer fabric*
- *¼" (0.6 cm) diameter wood dowel*
- *1" X 1" (2.5 X 2.5 cm) wood mounting board*
- *2 decorative weights*
- *2 small L-brackets*
- *Marking pencil*
- *Staple gun*

## PROJECT TECHNIQUES

- *Double-Fold Hem (page 141)*
- *Topstitch (page 141)*

## Preparation

Use one width of fabric for the finished panel width. Measure the height from floor to ceiling. Subtract the length of the decorative weights. Add 2" (5.1 cm) for the bottom rod pocket plus 5" (12.7 cm) to wrap the wood mounting board at the ceiling.

The horizontal tucks can be spaced as desired. Calculate the number of tucks you'll need for the divider's finished height. Add 1" (2.5 cm) per tuck to the above measurement.

Cut one panel of sheer fabric the total height measurement by one width of fabric.

## Construction

**Step 1** Make a ½" (1.2 cm)-wide double-fold hem along each side edge.

**Step 2** To form a rod pocket for the bottom of the divider, press ½" (1.2 cm) to the wrong side of the bottom edge. Fold again to make a ¾" (1.9 cm)-wide finished hem and topstitch near the inner folded edge.

**Step 3** Measure and mark the tuck placements on the right side of the fabric. Fold the fabric horizontally at one of the tuck placement lines, with the wrong sides together. Stitch ½" (1.2 cm) from the fold from side to side of the fabric. Repeat for each tuck.

**Step 4** Cut the 1" X 1" (2.5 X 2.5 cm) wood mounting board length to ½" (1.2 cm) less than the finished width of the panel. Cover the ends with the shade fabric. Staple the top of the panel to one side of the wood mounting board. Wrap all four sides, and then turn the board once more, so that the upper raw edge of the fabric is completely encased.

**Step 5** Attach the decorative weights to the bottom corners of the panel.

**Step 6** Insert the wood dowel rod into the bottom rod pocket. Attach the L-brackets to the ceiling and the ends of the wood mounting board to the brackets.

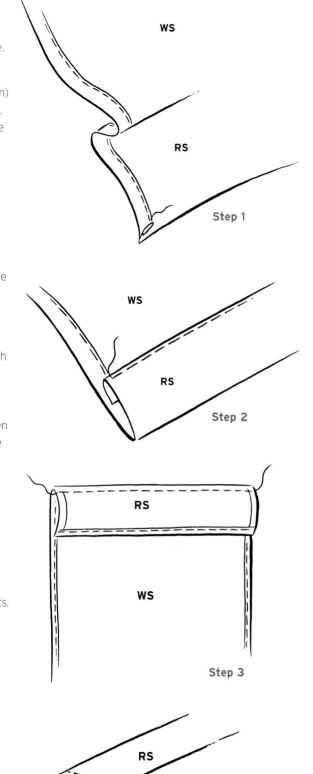

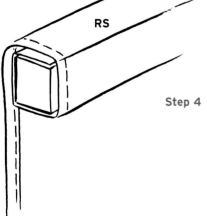

# Trimmed Door Panels

OUTDOOR CURTAINS, used for insulation or privacy, are nicely detailed with wide flat bands. The fabric border frame stabilizes the heavy curtain and adds subtle sophistication.

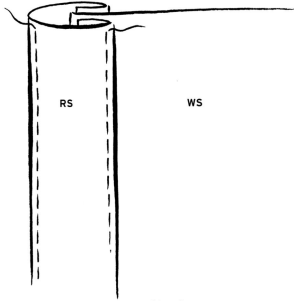

RS

WS

Step 3

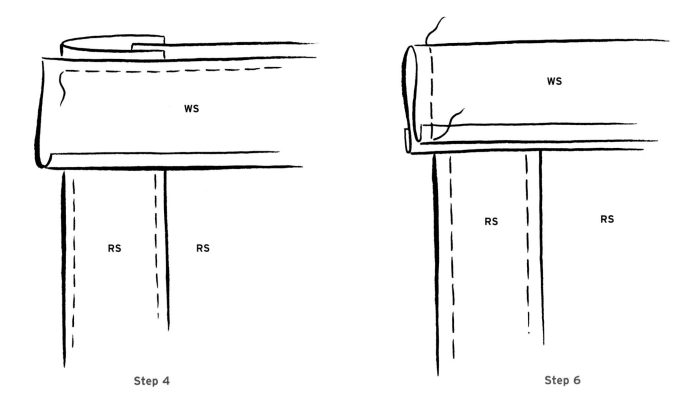

WS

RS          RS

Step 4

WS

RS          RS

Step 6

## MATERIALS

- *Weatherproof fabric for the curtains*
- *Weatherproof fabric for the bands*
- *Curtain rings*
- *Curtain rod and mounting hardware*
- *Heavy-duty snaps for the tiebacks*
- *Tool kit to set the snaps*

## PROJECT TECHNIQUES

- *Topstitch (page 141)*
- *Seam Positions for Fabric Widths (page 148)*

## Preparation

Measure the width of the space to be covered with fabric. Multiply by 1.5 for fullness. Divide the total width in half to make two panels. Add 1" (2.5 cm) for seam allowances.

Measure the length of the space to be covered. Subtract 6" (15.2 cm) for bands and add 1" (2.5 cm) for seam allowances on both sides.

Cut two panels of curtain fabric to the height and width as measured. Join fabric widths if needed.

Cut four strips of band fabric, each 7" (17.8 cm)-wide by the cut length of the curtain panel for the side borders.

Cut four strips of band fabric, each 7" (17.8 cm) -wide by the cut width of the curtain panel plus 6" (15.2 cm) for the top and bottom borders.

Experiment to determine the length of the tiebacks and cut four pieces of fabric to the desired length X 5½" (14 cm).

## Construction

**Step 1** Press ½" (1.2 cm) to the wrong side along the long edges of the bands.

**Step 2** With right sides together, sew the unpressed edge of one band to each side of a panel, aligning the bands even with the top and bottom of the curtain panel. Press the bands away from the panel with the seam allowances toward the band.

**Step 3** Fold each band to the wrong side, with the unattached edge covering the seam allowances and just covering the seamline. Press the band. Topstitch ¼" (0.6 cm) from the inner and outer edges of the bands.

**Step 4** With right sides together, sew the unpressed edge of the top and bottom bands to the curtain panel, extending them ½" (1.2 cm) beyond each end.

**Step 5** Fold the bands to the wrong side, with the unattached edge covering the seam allowances and just covering the seamline. Press the band.

**Step 6** Temporarily refold the bands in half with right sides together. Sew a ½" (1.2 cm) seam allowance at each end of the bands, to close the corners.

**Step 7** Turn the bands to the outside. Topstitch ¼" (0.6 cm) from the inner and outer edges of the bands.

**Step 8** With right sides together, sew two tieback pieces together using a ½" (1.2 cm) seam allowance and leaving an opening for turning. Trim the seams and corners. Turn each tieback to the outside and press the seam allowances of the opening to the inside. Topstitch ¼" (0.6 cm) from all edges.

**Step 9** Install a snap according to the manufacturer's recommendations on each tieback.

**Step 10** Clamp or sew the curtain rings to the top of the panel. Thread the panel on to a curtain rod and install the rod.

# Eyelet Draperies

ALTERNATIVE DRAPERY HEADINGS are very popular. This use of large eyelets, also called grommets, make quick work of softly pleating the top of drapery panels.

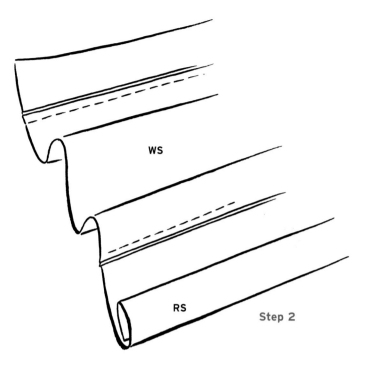

WS

RS

Step 2

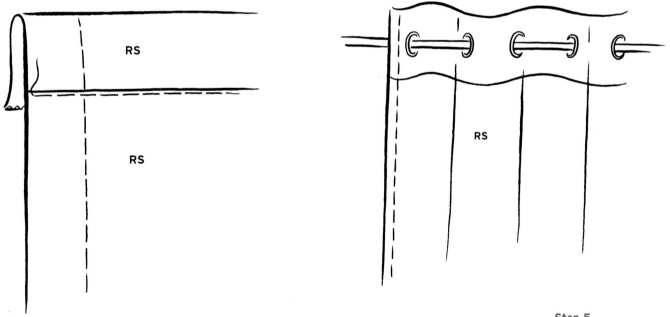

RS

RS

Step 4

RS

Step 5

## MATERIALS

**Note:** *The following instructions are for one panel. Repeat the process to make a set.*

- *Fabric*
- *Contrasting fabric for top and bottom accents*
- *Curtain rod and mounting hardware*
- *Large eyelets and installation tool kit*

## PROJECT TECHNIQUES

- *Finish (page 141)*
- *Stitch-in-the-Ditch (page 141)*
- *Topstitch (page 141)*
- *Seam Positions for Fabric Widths (page 148)*
- *Puddling (page 150)*

## Preparation

Measure the length and width of the window. Divide this in half, for a single panel. For fullness, allow two times the width. Add 6" (15.2 cm) total for the side hems.

For the panel's total length, start with the finished length from the top of the window to the floor. Add 2" (5.1 cm) for puddling, 4½" (11.4 cm) for the top hem, and 8" (20.3 cm) for the bottom hem. Subtract 20 percent of the length determined to this point for the bottom contrasting fabric accent depth. Subtract 9" (22.9 cm) for the top contrasting accent fabric, and add 1" (2.5 cm) for the seam allowances.

Sew widths of fabric sections together to make a panel to the final length and width measurements as determined above.

Cut a contrasting fabric accent length to 20 percent of the panel's finished length (from the top of the window to the floor, plus 2" (5.1 cm), plus 8" (20.3 cm), plus 4½" (11.4 cm).

Add a ½" (1.2 cm) seam allowance and an 8" (20.3 cm) hem allowance. Make the width to match the final panel's width for the bottom accent.

Cut a contrasting fabric accent length to 9½" (24.1 cm) and the same width as the final panel's width for the top accent.

## Construction

**Step 1** With right sides together, sew the narrower top and longer bottom contrasting fabric sections to the body of the fabric panel. Press the seam allowances toward the accent fabric pieces.

**Step 2** Make a 4" (10 cm)-deep double-fold hem.

**Step 3** Make 1½" (3.8 cm)-wide double-fold side hems.

**Step 4** Finish the top edge of the drapery panel. Turn the top edge to the wrong side 4½" (11.4 cm) and press. Stitch-in-the-ditch of the seam for the contrasting fabric accent to catch the hem on the wrong side.

**Step 5** Mark the locations of the eyelet placements, no more than 8" (20.3 cm) apart, along the top contrasting fabric accent section. Position the last eyelet at each end 1½" (3.8 cm) in from the finished side edges. Using a tool provided by the manufacturer, install the eyelets.

**Step 6** To hang the two panels, thread the curtain rod through the eyelets and install the rod on corresponding brackets.

# Tapered Valance

THIS EASY-TO-MAKE gathered valance consists of a scalloped center panel and separate cascading side pieces. The rickrack trim is a clever edge treatment.

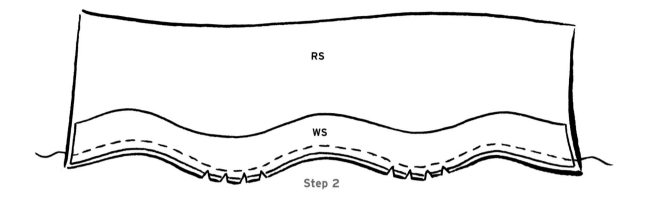

RS

WS

Step 2

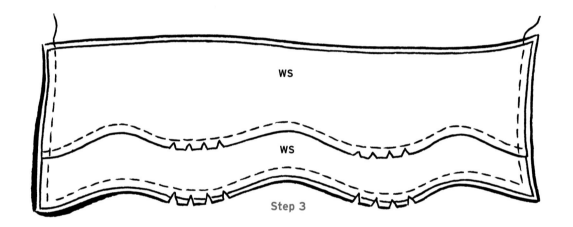

WS

WS

Step 3

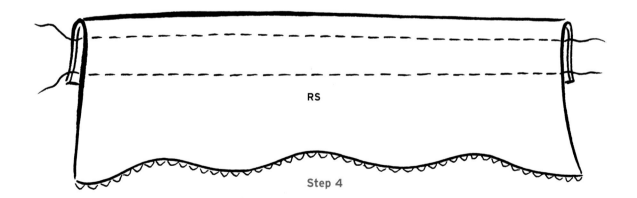

RS

Step 4

## MATERIALS

- *Fabric*
- *Lining fabric*
- *Rickrack trim*
- *Curtain rod for each center and side panel set*
- *Pattern paper*

## PROJECT TECHNIQUES

- *Baste (page 141)*
- *Finish (page 141)*
- *Topstitch (page 141)*
- *Seam Positions for Fabric Widths (page 148)*

## Center Panel Preparation

Measure the width of the window.

Calculate the fullness at 3 times the finished width of the window.

Make the center panel 12" (30.5 cm) to 18" (45.7 cm)-long or as desired.

Make a paper pattern for one-half of the total width. Add 6½" (16.5 cm) at the top for the heading and the rod pocket. Draw two parallel lines, at the bottom of the panel, as guides for making the highest and lowest points of the scallop edging. Draw the desired number of scallops between the two bottom horizontal lines. Add ½" (1.2 cm) seam allowances to the bottom and outer vertical edge of the paper pattern. (The opposite vertical edge is cut on fold.)

Join fabric widths together as needed. Cut one fabric valance twice as wide as the paper pattern.

Mark a line 5" (12.7 cm) above the bottom scalloped edge of the paper pattern, for the facing.

Cut one fabric facing piece.

Cut one lining piece the size of the valance pattern minus the facing piece plus 1" (2.5 cm) at the bottom.

## Side Panels Preparation

Use one-half width of fabric for the side panels.

Calculate the side panel at two-thirds longer than the center panel's finished length. Add 6½" (16.5 cm) for the heading.

Make a paper pattern one-half of the fabric width by the length of the side panel plus seam allowances.

At the center edge (the inner edge, which is nearest the center panel) round the bottom corner. Add ½" (1.2 cm) seam allowances to the sides and bottom.

Cut two fabric pieces for the side panels, reversing the pattern for one piece, to make the opposite side.

Mark a line 5" (12.7 cm) from the bottom edge and inner vertical edge for the facing cutting line.

Cut two fabric facing pieces, reversing the pattern for one piece.

Cut two lining pieces to the size of the side panel pattern minus the facing piece plus 1" (2.5 cm) at the bottom edge.

## Center Panel Construction

**Step 1** On the right side of the fabric, center the rickrack trim on the bottom seamline of the center panel. Baste it in place.

**Step 2** With right sides together, sew the facing to the lining and press the seam allowances toward the lining, clipping the seam allowances along the curves as needed.

**Step 3** With right sides together, sew the facing/lining piece to the valance piece along the bottom and sides, using the previous trim stitching line as a guide.

**Step 4** Turn the valance to the outside and press the edges. Finish the top edges together. Turn the top 5" (12.7 cm) to the wrong side. Topstitch a line 1" (2.5 cm) from the top edge to form a heading and another line 3" (7.6 cm) from the top to make the rod casing.

## Side Panels Construction

**Step 1** On the right side of the fabric, center the rickrack trim on the bottom seam allowance line of each side panel. Baste it in place.

**Step 2** Repeat steps 2 through 4 of the center panel instructions for each of the side panels.

**Step 3** Feed the curtain rod through the casing openings of the right side panel, the center panel, and the left side panel. Allow 2" (5.1 cm) of each side panel to wrap the rod as returns.

# Double Fold Panels

UNUSUALLY SHAPED WINDOWS can be given a valance when the window treatment is created by folding fabric. Buttons form the pleats and the window is dressed with simple semi-sheer curtains. In an instant, the valance can be loosely hung by rings that are mounted on a small iron rod.

## MATERIALS

- *Fabric (both sides of fabric will show)*
- *Curtain rod and mounting supplies*
- *Curtain rings*
- *Shank buttons*

## PROJECT TECHNIQUES

- *Buttons (page 140)*
- *Topstitch (page 141)*
- *Double-Fold Hem (page 141)*
- *Seam Positions for Fabric Widths (page 148)*

## Preparation

Measure the width and height of the area to be covered.

To calculate the total finished width of one panel, divide in half the width of the area to be covered. Multiply by two for fullness. Add 2" (5.1 cm) for side hems.

Calculate one-fourth of the finished length and add that amount to the length for the folded valance. Add 11" (27.9 cm) total to the length for the top and bottom hems.

Join widths of fabric together as needed.

Cut two panels of fabric to the final width and length measurements.

## Construction

**Step 1** Press ½" (1.2 cm) to the wrong side of the bottom of each panel. Press an additional 5" (12.7 cm) to the wrong side for the hem. Topstitch along the inner fold.

**Step 2** Press ½" (1.2 cm) to the right side of the top of each panel, Press an additional 5" (12.7 cm) to the right side for the top hem. Topstitch along the inner fold.

**Step 3** Press ½" (1.2 cm) to the wrong side of both sides of each panel. Press another ½" (1.2 cm) to the wrong side to make ½" (1.2 cm) double-fold side hems.

**Step 4** Fold the valance portion to the right side of the panel.

**Step 5** Pin-mark along the fold to mark off even spaces approximately every 8" (20.3 cm), starting about 3" (7.6 cm) from each side. Pinch the double layer of fabric together at each pin-mark. Measure 2" (5.1 cm) down from the top and sew a button on each side of the pleat, back to back, so that the sewing thread holding the buttons together secures the pleat.

**Step 6** Sew a curtain ring to the top of both panels, at each pleat. Thread the curtain rod through all of the rings, and then install the window treatment.

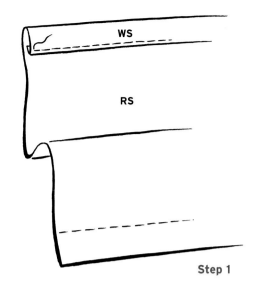

Step 1

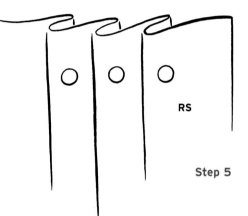

Step 5

# Knotted Tab Bed Panels

FOR STYLE AND ELEGANCE, these tied bed hangings for a four-poster bed have no equal. They are also simple to make using sheer, natural fabric such as gauze. This same look also works well as a window treatment.

## MATERIALS

**Note:** *The following instructions are for one panel. Repeat for each panel.*

• *Fabric*

## PROJECT TECHNIQUES
• *Double-Fold Hem (page 141)*
• *Fabric Tubes (page 142)*
• *Seam Positions for Fabric Widths (page 148)*

## Preparation

Determine the finished length of the ties by experimenting with a scrap of fabric tied over the top of the upper bed rail.

Determine the length of the bed panels by measuring the distance from the upper bed rail to the floor, adding 5" (12.7 cm) for top and hem allowances and 2" (5.1 cm) for puddling. Subtract the finished length of the tie.

Measure the width of the bed opening where one panel will hang. Divide this measurement in half, for two panels along one side. Double the measurement for the cut width of a panel and add 2" (5.1 cm) for side hems.

Sew fabric widths together to achieve the total width for each panel. Cut the panel lengths to the measurements as determined.

Cut strips of fabric 3" (7.6 cm) -wide by the width of each finished panel plus two ½" (1.2 cm) seam allowances for the top facings.

Cut strips of fabric 3" (7.6 cm) -wide X length needed for each tie. Plan to place one pair of ties approximately every 8" (20.3 cm).

## Construction

**Step 1** At the lower edge of each panel, turn ½" (1.2 cm) to the wrong side and press the fold. Turn an additional 4" (10 cm) to the wrong side, press it, and then topstitch along the inner edge of the fold.

**Step 2** Make a 1" (2.5 cm)-wide double-fold hem at both sides. Stitch next to the inner fold.

**Step 3** To make a tie, fold the strips with right sides together and stitch the long edges together and across one short end. Trim the seams and turn the tie to the outside. Repeat for all the remaining ties.

**Step 4** Beginning at one end of a panel, approximately every 8" (20.3 cm) pin the raw ends of two ties to the right side at the top of the panel.

**Step 5** Press one long edge and the two short ends of the facing ½" (1.2 cm) to the wrong side. Pin the unpressed edge of the facing to the right side of the top of the panel, sandwiching the ties between the facing and the panel. Stitch through all layers, also securing the ties in the seamline.

**Step 6** Turn the facing to the wrong side and topstitch all the edges of the facing to the panel.

**Step 7** Tie the panels to the bed rails, allowing the panels to puddle about 2" (5.1 cm) on the floor.

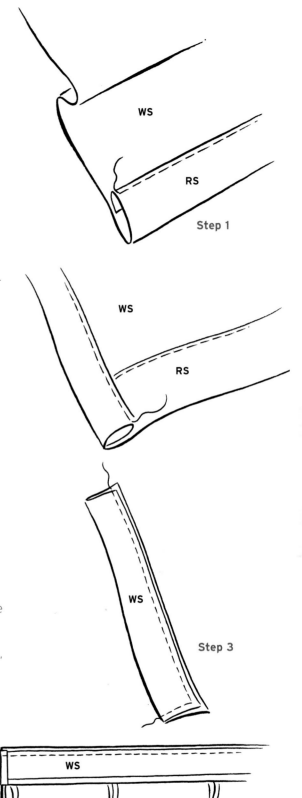

WS

RS

Step 1

WS

RS

WS

Step 3

WS

RS

Step 5

# Bordered Tablecloth

TWO PRETTY FABRICS, a mini-print and a summer stripe, are the perfect complements for a bright, weather-resistant tablecloth. The wide border frames the tablecloth and forms a bold mitered corner.

# Shirred Vanity Skirt

A KIDNEY-SHAPED VANITY TABLE is all dressed up with a double layer skirt made from embroidered cotton voile placed over a solid cotton fabric. The layers are shirred at the top and tassel-trimmed at the bottom.

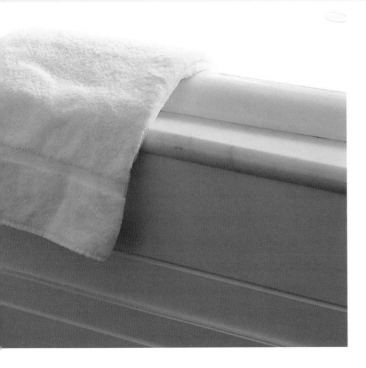

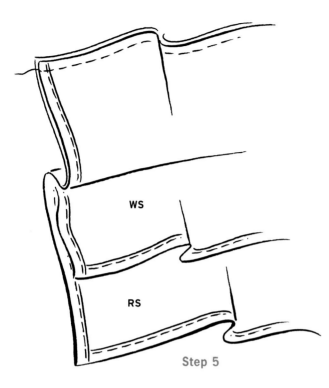

WS

RS

Step 5

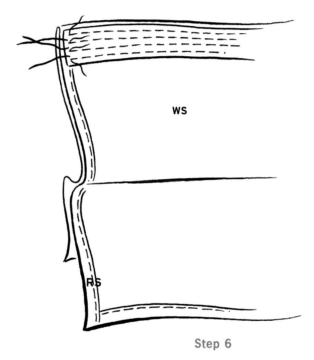

WS

RS

Step 6

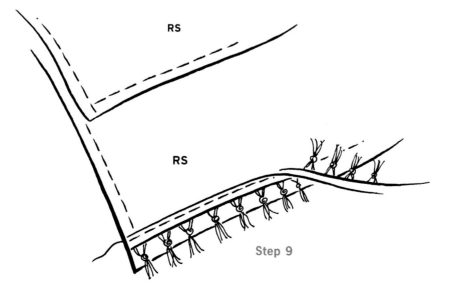

RS

RS

Step 9

## MATERIALS

- *Embroidered sheer fabric, such as cotton voile*
- *Solid-color fabric*
- *Tassel trim*
- *3" (7.6 cm)-wide 3-pleat pleating tape*
- *Glue*
- *Hook-and-loop tape with adhesive backing*

## PROJECT TECHNIQUES

- *Topstitch (page 141)*
- *Seam Positions for Fabric Widths (page 148)*

## Preparation

Measure the circumference of the table and double the number for fullness.

Measure the height of the table and add 2½" (6.4 cm) for seam and hem allowances.

Using the width and height measurements, cut enough widths of solid-color fabric to make a single panel that will be wrapped around the entire table. Using the solid-color fabric piece measurements, cut enough sheer fabric panels to make the same width by the height less 8" (20.3 cm).

Cut a length of pleating tape the width of the finished skirt.

Cut a length of tassel trim the width of the finished skirt plus 2" (5.1 cm).

## Construction

**Step 1** Sew the widths of solid-color fabric together to make one complete solid-color panel. Press the seam allowances open. Sew the widths of sheer fabric together to make one complete sheer panel. Press the seam allowances open.

**Step 2** Press 1" (2.5 cm) of the bottom hem allowance to the wrong side of the solid skirt and press. Turn the raw edge to meet the pressed fold and press again. Stitch close to the second fold.

**Step 3** Repeat step 2 to make side hems on the solid-color skirt.

**Step 4** Repeat steps 2 and 3 to hem the sheer skirt.

**Step 5** With right side of the sheer fabric against the wrong side of the solid-color fabric, sew the sheer skirt to the solid skirt at the top using a ½" (1.2 cm) seam allowance. Press the seam allowances open and then turn the sheer skirt to the outside, over the solid skirt, and press.

**Step 6** Pin the top of the pleating tape ¼" (0.6 cm) down from the top of the layered skirt. Pull out ½" (1.2 cm) of each cord at both ends. Turn the tape under to finish the ends, making sure that the pleating tape cords are not included in the fabric that is folded under. Secure the length of pleating tape to the top of the skirt, through all of the fabric layers, by stitching along the top and bottom of the tape and between each row of cord.

**Step 7** At one edge, make a knot in the end of each cord in the tape. Apply glue to the knots to keep in place. Trim the ends.

**Step 8** Pull the other ends of the cords until the skirt gathers up to the finished width. Knot, glue, and trim the pulled cord ends.

**Step 9** Pin the tassel trim to the solid skirt hem, wrapping both ends of the braid to the wrong side. Attach the tassel trim by stitching through the braid.

**Step 10** Hand tack the hook side of the hook-and-loop tape to the pleating tape on the wrong side of the skirt.

**Step 11** Adhere the loop side of the hook-and-loop tape to the apron of the table. Align the two sides of the hook-and-loop tape to install the skirt on the table.

# Ottoman Slipcover

A GREAT PIECE OF FABRIC and some simple sewing can quickly change the look or season of a square or rectangular ottoman.

## MATERIALS

• *Fabric*

## PROJECT TECHNIQUES

• *Finish (page 141)*
• *Topstitch (page 141)*

## Preparation

Measure the width and length of the top of the ottoman.

Cut one piece of fabric to the top measurement plus 1" (2.5 cm) seam allowances on all four sides.

Measure the height and width of the sides.

Cut four pieces of fabric to the height and width measurement of the sides. Add ½" (1.2 cm) seam allowances to the top and sides. Add 1" (2.5 cm) to the bottom for the hem allowance.

## Construction

**Step 1** With right sides together, sew the top edge of one side to the corresponding edge of the top. Start and stop stitching ½" (1.2 cm) from each end. Press the seam allowances and side away from the top.

**Step 2** Sew the adjacent side to the top, starting at the previous stitching and stopping ½" (1.2 cm) from the other end. Do not sew through the previous side piece. Again press the seam allowances and side away from the top.

**Step 3** Continue to sew all sides to the top.

**Step 4** Temporarily fold the seam allowances toward the top. With right sides together, match the raw edges of two adjacent sides at a corner. Sew from the last stitch of the previous seam to the bottom raw edge. Press the corner seam allowances toward the sides. Repeat for each corner.

**Step 5** Finish the bottom raw edge of the slipcover. Turn the bottom edge to the wrong side 1" (2.5 cm) and topstitch.

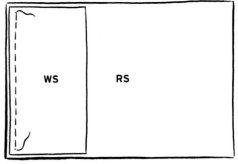

Step 1

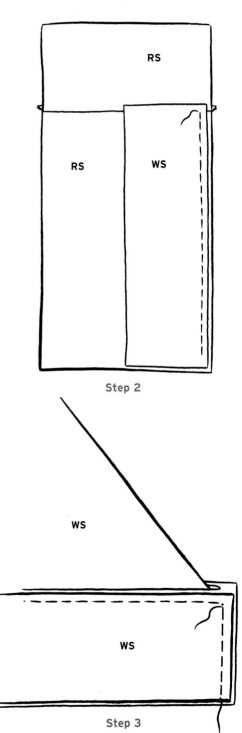

Step 2

Step 3

# Headboard Slipcover

TURN A SMALL WOOD-FRAMED BED into a daybed or banquette
by adding a tie-on padded slipcover at the headboard, footboard,
or both. The use of neutral-colored linen fabric encourages extra
accessorizing with collectable ethnic-style pillows.

## MATERIALS

- *Fabric*
- *Polyester batting*
- *Temporary spray adhesive*

## PROJECT TECHNIQUES

- *Edgestitch (page 141)*
- *Slipstitch (page 141)*
- *Topstitch (page 141)*

**Note:** These instructions produce two padded, fabric-covered forms that tie to both sides of a head or footboard.

## Preparation

Measure the width and length of the desired area to be covered on the headboard. Add ½" (1.2 cm) seam allowances to all sides and cut four pieces of fabric. Two cut pieces are for the faces and two are for the linings.

Cut two pieces of polyester batting the same size as a face fabric piece.

Determine the length of a fabric tie needed to wrap around the wood frame, adding length for a bow and ½" (1.2 cm) seam allowances on all sides. Cut 18 pieces of fabric, 2" (5.1 cm)-wide by the desired length for tie plus a total of 1" (2.5 cm) for seam allowances at the short ends.

## Construction

**Step 1** Spray the wrong side of two lining fabric pieces with temporary spray adhesive and adhere a piece of batting to each lining.

**Step 2** Fold ½" (1.2 cm) at one short end of a tie to the wrong side. Press it in half lengthwise, with the wrong sides together.

**Step 3** Unfold the tie and press each raw edge to the center foldline. Again fold the tie in half lengthwise. Edgestitch along all the folded edges. Repeat to make the remaining ties.

**Step 4** Place two ties to the right side of the corners and one tie at each bottom corner. Center a tie on the top, and another on each of the two sides. Place the finished ends of the ties toward the center of the cover.

**Step 5** With right sides together, sew a face to a lining, leaving an opening along the bottom for turning.

**Step 6** Turn the slipcover to the right side and slipstitch the opening closed.

**Step 7** Topstitch ½" (1.2 cm) from the outer edge along all sides.

**Step 8** Using the remaining face, lining, and polyester batting pieces sew another slipcover. Place one slipcover on each side of the headboard and tie them together at the top and sides.

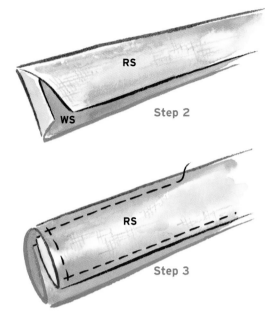

Step 2

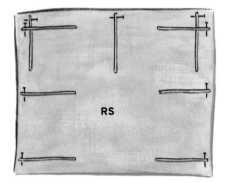

Step 3

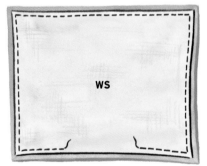

Step 4

Step 5

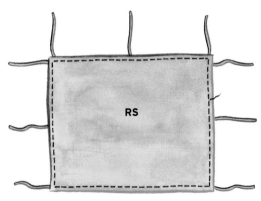

Step 7

# Chair Pads and Cozies

WOODEN CHAIRS are more comfortable with the addition
of padded seat cushions and back covers, called cozies.
A bright floral print adds color to a simple interior.

# Scalloped Skirt **Slipcover**

DRESS UP A CHAIR with a removable seat cover that is designed to be tied to the chair back. Self-lined half circles overlap one another to make a faux-scalloped trim for the lower edge.

# Envelope Duvet

CREATE AN OVERLAPPING, envelope-style button closure for a
duvet cover. This treatment allows easy access to the comforter
insert and adds a decorative touch for the well-dressed bed.

## MATERIALS

- Fabric for the duvet top and the top of the envelope flap
- Fabric for the duvet back
- Decorative trim with flange
- Buttons

## PROJECT TECHNIQUES

- Buttons (page 140)
- Topstitch (page 141)
- Attaching Twisted Cording (page 147)
- Seam Positions for Fabric Widths (page 148)

## Preparation

Using half the fabric yardage as noted in the Duvet Yardage Requirements chart below, cut two lengths of fabric. Join the fabric widths. Cut the seamed fabric to the finished measurements as noted in the table below, adding ½" (1.2 cm) seam allowances on all sides.

Cut four pieces of fabric, each 20" (50.8 cm)-long plus seam allowances X the full fabric width. Join two of the cut pieces of fabric to make two 20" (50.8 cm) long sections. Cut each of the joined pieces 20" (50.8 cm) by the finished duvet width plus ½" (1.2 cm) seam allowances on all sides, one for the envelope flap and one for the flap lining.

Cut two lengths of lining fabric the desired length of the duvet minus 20" (50.8 cm) plus 2" (5.1 cm) for underlap hem, for the duvet back. Add seam allowances on all sides. Join the fabric widths to make one lining piece.

Cut the twisted cord to the width of the envelope flap's long edge.

## Construction

**Step 1** Sew the twisted cord to the right side of one long edge of the envelope flap.

**Step 2** With right sides together, sew the envelope flap to the flap lining along the trimmed edge.

**Step 3** Turn the flap to the outside and baste the raw edges together. Stitch buttonholes 1" (2.5 cm) from—and perpendicular to—the trimmed edge, spacing them approximately 9" (22.9 cm) apart across the width.

**Step 4** On the underlap edge of the duvet back, press ½" (1.2 cm) to the wrong side. Press an additional 2" (5.1 cm) to the wrong side and topstitch along the inner, folded edge.

**Step 5** Pin the flap over the duvet back, placing the buttonholes over the hemmed underlap edge. Baste the layers together along the side seams.

**Step 6** Sew buttons to the underlap hem in positions that correspond with the buttonholes on the flap.

**Step 7** With right sides together, sew the duvet front to the back along all four sides. Turn the duvet to the outside and insert the comforter. Button the envelope flap closed.

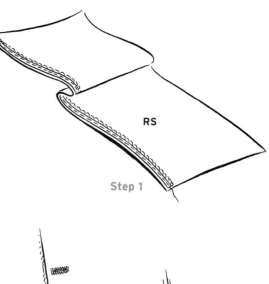

Step 1

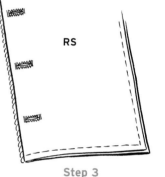

Step 3

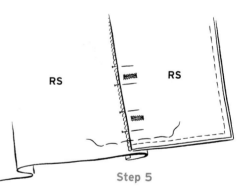

Step 5

These measurements are for one side only. The figure in parentheses is the number of extra repeats per side.

| BED SIZE | TWIN | DOUBLE | QUEEN | KING |
|---|---|---|---|---|
| | 39" X 75" (99 X 191 cm) | 54" X 75" (137 X 191 cm) | 60" X 80" (152 X 203 cm) | 76" X 80" (193 X 203 cm) |

### Duvet Yardage Requirements

| BED SIZE | | TWIN | DOUBLE | QUEEN | KING |
|---|---|---|---|---|---|
| FABRIC WIDTH | 44"/45" (111.8 cm/114.3 cm) | 5 yards (4.5 m) (1) | 5 yards (4.5 m) (1) | 5½ yards (5 m) (1) | 8 yards (7.6 m) (2) |
| | 54" (137 cm) | 5 yards (4.5 m) (1) | 5 yards (4.5 m) (1) | 5½ yards (5 m) (1) | 5½ yards (5 m) (1) |

# Mattress Bench Cushion

A FOAM CUSHION, WHEN TUFTED with big stitches around all
of the edges, is a casual alternative to a traditional box treatment.
The technique will work for any size cushion: from a large bench to
a small pillow.

## MATERIALS

- Fabric
- 5" (12.7 cm)-thick foam cushion
- Perle cotton or heavy thread
- Hand sewing needle
- Marking pencil
- Upholstery needle

## PROJECT TECHNIQUES

- Slipstitch (page 141)

## Preparation

Measure the width and length of the opening for the cushion and subtract 1" (2.5 cm). Cut two pieces of fabric to the measurements, plus ½" (1.2 cm) seam allowances on all sides, for the cushion top and bottom.

Cut four strips of fabric, each 7" (17.8 cm)-wide and the same length as the cushion top for the boxings. Cut the foam cushion to the finished size of the bench cushion.

## Construction

**Step 1** With right sides together and using ½" (1.2 cm) seam allowances, sew the boxing sides to the front at the short ends. Continue joining boxing strips together to form a continuous strip.

**Step 2** With right sides together and matching the boxing seams to the corners, sew one long edge of the boxing to the cushion top. Clip the seam allowances at each corner to enable the fabric to turn the corner. (See step 3 of the Box Pillow instructions on page 99.)

**Step 3** Sew the remaining edge of the boxing to the cushion bottom, leaving an opening along one edge for turning. Turn the cover to the outside.

**Step 4** Insert the foam cushion and slipstitch the opening closed.

**Step 5** Mark dots 2" (5.1 cm) apart along each edge of the top, the bottom and the boxing, placing them 1½" (3.8 cm) from the seams.

**Step 6** To tuft the edges, thread an upholstery needle with perle cotton. Insert the needle through the first mark on the cushion top and bring the needle out through the foam and the corresponding mark on the boxing. Leave the end about 2" (5.1 cm)-long. Insert the needle about ¼" (0.6 cm) away from the first stitch, through the boxing and foam and out the top about ¼" (0.6 cm) from the starting point. Knot together the thread ends tightly and trim the ends to 1" (2.5 cm)-long. Repeat for all the markings.

**Step 7** Mark the top and bottom in an evenly spaced grid approximately 8" (20.3 cm) apart. Continue tufting by pulling the needle and thread down through the top, out the bottom, and then back up to the top.

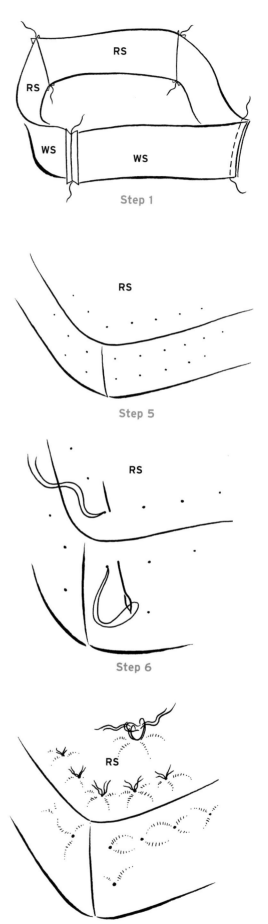

# Button-Back Slipcover

SLIPCOVERS HIDE BLEMISHES, protect furniture from spills, and add charm to dining room chairs like the ones shown here. Using simple rectangles of fabric, this style of slipcover can be measured and cut to fit any size chair, and it is easy to assemble. The button detail on the back adds interest and simplifies its installation.

# HOW TO MEASURE A CHAIR FOR A SLIPCOVER

Taking each measurement at the widest point of the chair, record the dimensions according to the following explanations.

## Inside Back

TOP WIDTH = the top edge from the back of side struts **(A)**.

BOTTOM WIDTH = the bottom edge at the seat from the back of side struts **(D)**.

HEIGHT = from the top of the seat, to the back of the top strut **(B)**.

## Seat

BACK WIDTH = edge to edge of the seat top **(E)**.

FRONT WIDTH = edge to edge of the seat top **(F)**.

DEPTH = the side edge from seat front to back **(G)**.

## Outside Back

RIGHT BACK = the top width from center back to corner **(H)** plus 3".

LEFT BACK = the top width from center back to corner **(H)** plus 3" (8 cm).

CENTER WIDTH = the back edge at seat **(I)**.

BOTTOM WIDTH = the back edge at seat **(I)** plus 2 pleats, 3" (8 cm) each.

HEIGHT = the top of the back to the bottom of skirt. (The skirt ends approximately halfway down the leg) **(B + C)**.

TOTAL OUTSIDE BACK =

## Front skirt

WIDTH = the front edge of the seat from corner to corner **(F)** plus two pleats, 3" (8 cm) each.

HEIGHT = from the top edge of seat to the bottom of the skirt **(C)**.

## Side skirt

WIDTH = from the side edge of the seat from the corner to the back of the chair **(G)** plus six pleats, 3" (8 cm) each.

HEIGHT = from the top edge of the seat to the bottom of the skirt **(C)**.

### Pattern Pieces

Draw the pattern pieces on paper for the inside back, seat, outside back, front skirt, and side skirt. To all edges, add ½" (1.2 cm) seam allowances. Add 1 ½" (3.8 cm) hem allowances to the front skirt, side skirts, and back.

Cut all pieces from the fabric. Clip a notch in the seam allowance at the top of each pleat line.

Make enough welting to sew to the top and two sides of inside back.

(Calculated the amount of welting by adding the width of the back **(H)** to the height of back **(B)** and multiplying by two. Also add 1" (2.5 cm) for seaming.) Make enough welting to sew to the top and two sides of inside back.

**Inside Back**

**Seat**

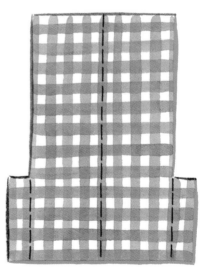

**Outside Back**

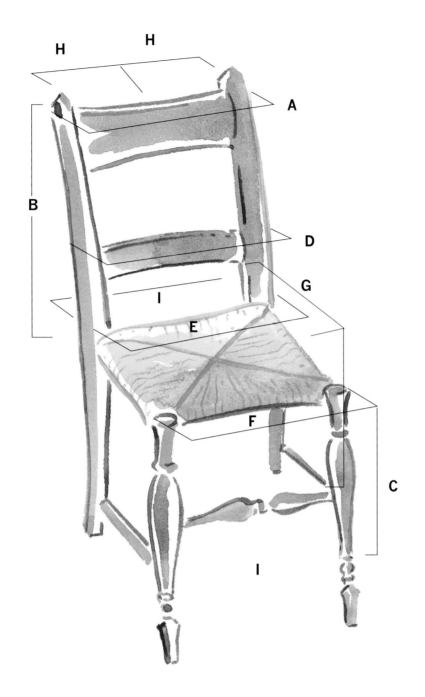

**Front Skirt**

**Side Skirt**

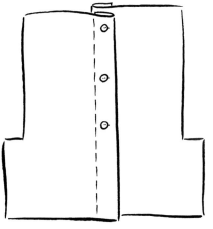

Step 4

Step 6

Step 7

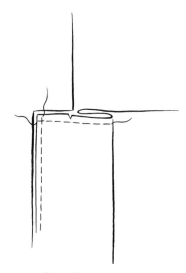

Step 8

Step 9

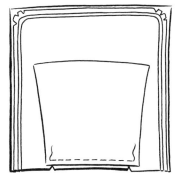

Step 11

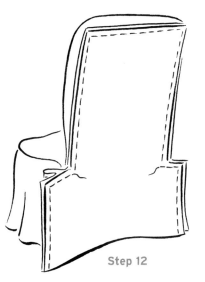

Step 12

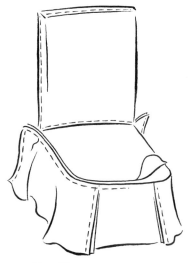

Step 13

## MATERIALS

- *Fabric*
- *Cording to cover*
- *Buttons*

## PROJECT TECHNIQUES

- *Attaching Sew-through Buttons (page 140)*
- *Making Covered Piping (page 145)*

## Construction

**Step 1** Finish the left edge (center) of the right outside back piece. Press 1½" (3.8 cm) to the wrong side. Topstitch the fold back.

**Step 2** Press 1½" (3.8 cm) to the wrong side of the right (center) edge of the left outside back. Press 1½" (3.8 cm) to the wrong side again to make a finished 1½" (3.8 cm)-wide double-fold hem. Topstitch along the length of the inner fold.

**Step 3** Make three buttonholes along the left back hem.

**Step 4** Place the left back over on the right back at the center so that the width across the two pieces is equal to the total width of the chair's outside back, plus 1" (2.5 cm). Baste the backs together across the top and bottom. Sew the corresponding buttons to the vertical hem of the right back piece.

**Step 5** With right sides together, sew one side edge of the front skirt to a side edge of one of the side skirts.

**Step 6** Join the other side edge of the front skirt to the side edge of other skirt in the same way.

**Step 7** Sew the other side edges of the side skirts to the side edges of the pleat extensions on the lower portion of the outside back pleat extensions.

**Step 8** Working from the right side of the skirt, make a 3" (7.6 cm) -wide box pleat at each corner, allowing the seam to become one of the crease in a back pleat. Baste each pleat in place.

**Step 9** Use a dart miter, as explained in this step, to box the top inside back corners. With the seamed fabric pieces wrong side out, position the partially assembled slipcover on the chair back. Smooth and wrap the fabric over the edges. Pin the fabric together along the corner. The excess fabric will form a diagonal fold. Pin the fold to make a dart. Trim the excess fabric. Repeat at the opposite corner. Remove the cover from the chair and sew the corner darts as pinned.

**Step 10** Stitch the covered piping to the top and side edges of the inside back piece.

**Step 11** With right sides together, center the back edge of the seat piece on the bottom of the inside back piece. Starting and stopping ½" (1.2 cm) from each end and using a ½" (1.2 cm) seam allowance, stitch the seat to the inside back. Clip the seam allowance of the inside back to the first and last stitch of the seam.

**Step 12** With right sides together, sew the inside back to the outside back along the top and sides, leaving the back halves of the pleats free.

**Step 13** Sew the remaining edges of the seat to the skirt panels, starting and stopping at the line of the back seam.

**Step 14** Finish the raw edge of the entire skirt hem. Press the hem allowance to the wrong side and top-stitch it in place.

# Box Pillow

A SQUARE PILLOW with a buttoned center and boxing feels more tailored than the version that has only a front and back. This box version can be used as a toss pillow or as a floor pillow, but a special dimensional form—either polyester or down and feather—will be required.

## MATERIALS

- 1½ yards (1.4 m) fabric
- 4½ yards (4.1 m) cording to cover
- ½ yard (0.6 m) cordonnet or heavy thread
- 18" (45.7 cm) square boxed pillow form
- 2 buttons to cover, each 1¼" (3.2 cm) in diameter
- Upholstery needle

## PROJECT TECHNIQUES

- Buttons (page 140)
- Slipstitch (page 141)
- Making Covered Piping (page 145)

## Finished Size

18 " X 18 " (45.7 X 45.7 cm)

## Preparation

Cut two pieces of fabric 19" X 19" (48.3 X 48.3 cm) for the front and back.

Cut four pieces of fabric 3" X 19" (8.1 X 48.3 cm) for the boxing.

Cover two buttons.

Make 4½ yards (4.1 m) of covered piping.

## Construction

**Step 1** Starting in the center of one edge, sew the covered piping to the right side of all the edges on the front and back pieces.

**Step 2** With right sides together, sew the short ends of all four boxing strips together. Stitch each seam starting and ending ½" (1.2 cm) from the edges. Press the seam allowances open.

**Step 3** Place a boxing seam at one corner of the pillow front. With right sides together, sew one long edge of the boxing to the right side of the pillow, starting and stopping at each seam corner opening. Repeat for all the remaining sides.

**Step 4** With right sides together, sew the opposite long edges of the boxing to the pillow back, leaving an opening along one edge for turning.

**Step 5** Turn the pillow to the outside and insert the form. Slipstitch the opening closed.

**Step 6** Tie and knot one end of the cordonnet thread to the shank of one covered button and thread the other end of the cordonnet through an upholstery needle.

**Step 7** Insert the needle through the center of the pillow. Remove the needle and pull the thread taut. Tie the loose end of the cordonnet thread to the second button. Trim the excess cordonnet.

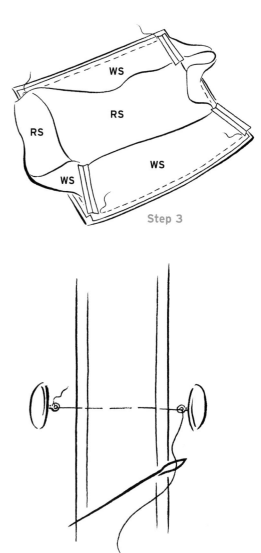

Step 3

Step 7

# Tied Pillow

THE FRONT DETAIL of this pillow is a designer variation of a tie closure. The knotted ties hold the pillow closed and allow an underlayer to peek through.

## MATERIALS

- 1½ yards (1.4 m) fabric
- 18" (45.7 cm) square pillow form
  2¼ yards (2 m) cording to cover

## PROJECT TECHNIQUES

- Fabric Tubes (page 142)
  Making Covered Piping
  (page 145)
- Joining Piping Ends (page 146)
  Fabric Ties (page 142)

## Finished Size

18" X 18" (45.7 X 45. 7 cm)

## Preparation

Cut one piece of 19" X 19" (48.3 X 48.3 cm) fabric for the pillow back.

Cut two pieces of 10" X 19" (25.4 X 48.3 cm) fabric for the pillow fronts.

Cut two pieces of 2½" (6.4 cm) X 19" (6.4 cm X 48.3 cm) fabric for the front facings.

Cut one piece of 4" X 19" (10 X 48.3 cm) fabric for the front underlay.

Cut six pieces of 1½" X 12" each (3.8 X 30.5 cm) fabric for the ties. Make 6 ties.

Make 2¼" yards (2 m) of covered piping.

## Construction

**Step 1** Place three ties on the right side of the center (long) edge of each pillow front, positioning one tie in the center, another 1" (2.5 cm) from the top, and another 1" (2.5 cm) from the bottom edge. Baste the ties in place.

**Step 2** With right sides together, stitch one facing to each pillow front, sandwiching the ties inside the fabric layers.

**Step 3** Butt the two faced front edges and place the right side of the underlayer on top of the facings, on the wrong side of the pillow. Baste across the top and bottom of all fabric layers.

**Step 4** Sew the covered piping to the outside edge of the pillow front.

**Step 5** With right sides together, sew the pillow front to the back. Turn the pillow to the outside and insert the pillow form. Knot the ties to close the front.

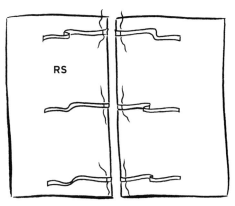

Step 1

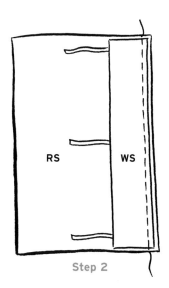

Step 2

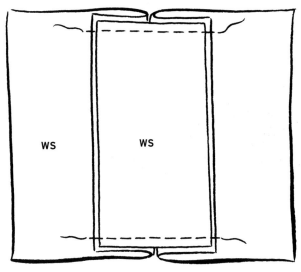

Step 3

# Pieced **Pillow**

THIS CHARMING PILLOW, shown resting against a bolster, features ethnic fabrics pieced in a simple block arrangement. The border is a quiet tonal fabric that has been accented with sashiko, which are small running stitches borrowed from an old Japanese hand sewing technique.

## MATERIALS

- ½ yard (0.5 m) light-color fabric for color blocks
- ¼ yard (0.23 m) dark-color contrasting fabric for color blocks
- ¼ yard (0.23 m) mid-tone solid-color fabric for accent strips
- 14" X 18" (35.6 X 45.7 cm) pillow form
- Cotton embroidery floss
- Hand sewing embroidery needle
- Walking foot

## PROJECT TECHNIQUES

- Slipstich (page141)

## Finished Size

14 " X 18" (35 .6 X 45.7 cm)

## Preparation

Cut ten pieces of light-color fabric, each 4⅝" X 7" (11.7 X 17.8 cm).

Cut eight pieces of dark-color contrasting fabric, each 4⅝" X 7" (11.7 X 17.8 cm).

Cut four pieces of mid-tone solid-color fabric, each 2½" X 19" (6.4 X 48.3 cm).

## Construction

**Step 1** With right sides together, using a walking foot, sew a light-color fabric piece to a long edge of a dark fabric piece. Sew another light-color fabric piece to the opposite edge. Press the seam allowances open. Repeat three more times to make a total of four color-blocked strips.

**Step 2** With right sides together, sew the remaining dark fabric pieces to the long edges of one light-color fabric piece. Repeat one more time to make a total of two pieced color-blocked strips. Press the seam allowances open.

**Step 3** Sew two pieced strips from step 1 to the long sides of a pieced strip from step 2 to make a pillow front. Repeat to make a pillow back. Press the seam allowances open.

**Step 4** With right sides together, sew the mid-tone solid-color strips to the top and bottom of the front and back. Press the seam allowances open.

**Step 5** Thread an embroidery needle with four plies of embroidery floss. On the mid-tone solid fabric, close to the seam, sew a line of running stitches about ¼" (0.6 cm) apart. Secure the thread at each end of the stitching.

**Step 6** With right sides together, sew the pillow front to the back, leaving an opening along one side to turn.

**Step 7** Turn the pillow to the outside and insert the form. Slipstitch the opening closed.

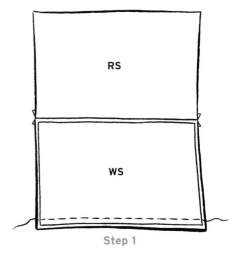

Step 1

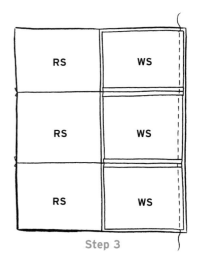

Step 3

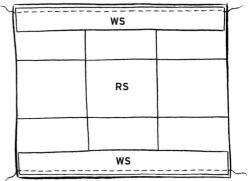

Step 4

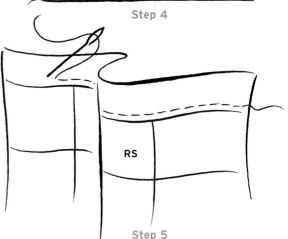

Step 5

## Tip

A SIMPLE WAY TO ACHIEVE A PIECED LOOK IS TO PURCHASE A FLAT WOVEN STRIPED RUG AND USE IT AS FABRIC TO MAKE A PILLOW. THIS APPROACH WAS USED FOR THE COORDINATING PILLOW SHOWN WITH THIS PROJECT.

# Pintuck Pillow

ADD SOPHISTICATED TEXTURE and dimension to the surface of a pillow with small tucks. They are sewn in a grid pattern on a solid fabric such as silk douppioni.

## MATERIALS

- 1⅕ yards (1.1 m) fabric for the pillow front and two overlapping backs
- 18" (45.7 cm) square pillow form
- Chalk marker
- Edgestitch presser foot

## PROJECT TECHNIQUES

- Edgestitch (page 141)
- Overlapping Closure (page 144)

## Finished Size

18" X 18" (45.7 X 45.7 cm)

## Preparation

Cut one piece of fabric 20" (50.8 cm) square for the pillow front.

Cut one piece of fabric 20" X 14" (50.8 cm X 35.6 cm) for the pillow back underlap.

Cut one piece of fabric 20" X 11½" (50.8 X 29.2 cm) for the pillow back overlap.

With the length along the grainline, cut four pieces of fabric 2" X 20" (5.1 X 50.8 cm)-wide 2" X 20" (5.1 X 50.8 cm)-long for the edge binding.

## Construction

**Step 1** Mark a vertical line along the center's right side. Mark another line 1¾" (4.5 cm) away on both sides of the center line. Moving toward the edges, mark parallel lines 3½" (8.9 cm) from these two lines.

**Step 2** With wrong sides together, fold the top along a marked line. Move the needle position 1⁄16" (0.2 cm) to the left. Using an edgestitch foot, stitch 1⁄16" (0.2 cm) from the fold. Repeat for each marked line.

**Step 3** Mark a center line on the right side of the pillow front, perpendicular to the previous stitching lines. Mark consecutive parallel lines 3½" (9 cm) away from the center line. Fold the pillow with the wrong sides together along the center line and stitch 1⁄16" (1.5 mm) from the fold. Repeat for each marked line.

**Step 4** Lay the pillow front flat and re-cut the piece to a 19" (48.3 cm) square.

**Step 5** Construct the pillow back using an overlapping closure.

**Step 6** With wrong sides together, sew the pillow front to the back. Trim the seam allowances to an even ½" (1.2 cm).

**Step 7** Fold and press one binding strip in half lengthwise. Open out the strip and press the raw edges to the center fold-line. Repeat for all strips.

**Step 8** Wrap a folded strip around a pillow front/back on seam allowance, encasing the raw edges. Edgestitch the folded strip, catching the front and back of the binding in the seam. Repeat on the opposite pillow edge. Trim the strips even with the upper and lower raw edges.

**Step 9** Apply the binding to the remaining, adjacent edges, finishing the raw edges of the strips by tucking them under.

**Step 10** Insert the pillow form through the overlapping back closure.

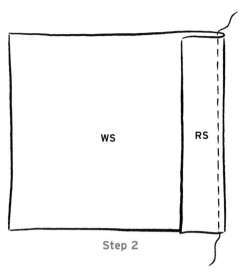

Step 2

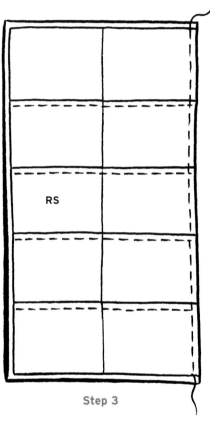

Step 3

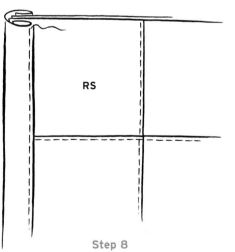

Step 8

# Sash Top **Pillow**

ACCENT A SQUARE PILLOW with button-on sashes. Combine two contrasting Asian-inspired fabrics or use a single Chinese brocade, flipping to the wrong side for the sashes.

Step 5

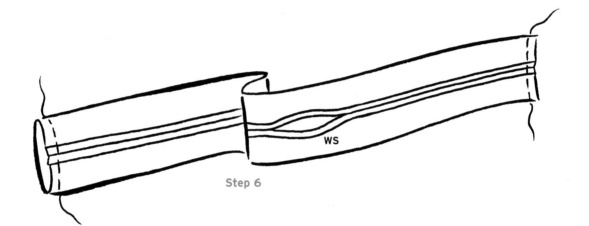

Step 6

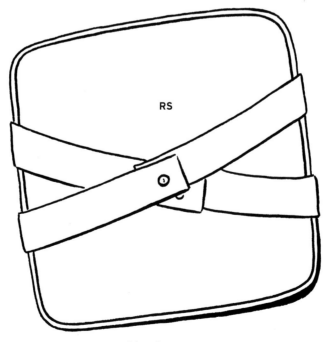

Step 9

## MATERIALS

- 1/2 yard (0.5 m) fabric for the pillow front and back
- 1 yard (0.9 m) of contrasting fabric for the piping and sashes
- 1/4 yard (0.2 m) cotton flannel
- 1 1/2 yards (1.4 m) cording to cover
- 18" (45.7 cm) square down pillow form
- 2 buttons

## PROJECT TECHNIQUES

- Buttons (page 140)
- Buttonholes (page 140)
- Slipstitch (page 141)
- Making Covered Piping (page 145)

## Finished Size

18" X 18"  (45.7 X 45. 7 cm)

## Preparation

Cut two pieces of pillow fabric 18" X 18" (45.7 X 45.7 cm) for the front and back.

Cut two pieces of contrasting fabric 6" X 40" (15.2 X 101.6 cm) for the sashes.

Cut two pieces of cotton flannel 6" X 40" (15.2 X 101.6 cm).

Make 2 1/4 yards (2 m) of covered cording.

## Construction

**Step 1** Starting at the center of one edge, sew the covered piping to the right side of the pillow front.

**Step 2** With right sides together, sew the pillow back to the front, leaving an opening for turning.

**Step 3** Turn the pillow to the outside and insert the pillow form. Slipstitch the opening closed.

**Step 4** Baste the cotton flannel to the wrong side of each sash.

**Step 5** With right sides together, fold a sash in half lengthwise and sew the long edges together, leaving an opening in the center for turning. Repeat for the remaining sash.

**Step 6** Center the seam along the length of the sash and press the seam allowances open. Stitch across each short end. Repeat for remaining sash.

**Step 7** Turn each sash to the outside and slipstitch the opening closed.

**Step 8** Loosely wrap each sash around the pillow with the seam side of the sash closest to the pillow. Overlap the sash ends on the back side of the pillow and determine the button and buttonhole location for each sash.

**Step 9** Sew a buttonhole at one end of each sash. Sew a button to correspond at the opposite end of each sash. Wrap the sashes around the pillow, crisscrossing them loosely, and button them together on the back side of the pillow.

# Drawstring Bolster

THIS TWO-TONE VELVET BOLSTER is trimmed in various combinations of decorative gimps and ribbons. The drawstring ends add charm and make the tubular cover easy to remove.

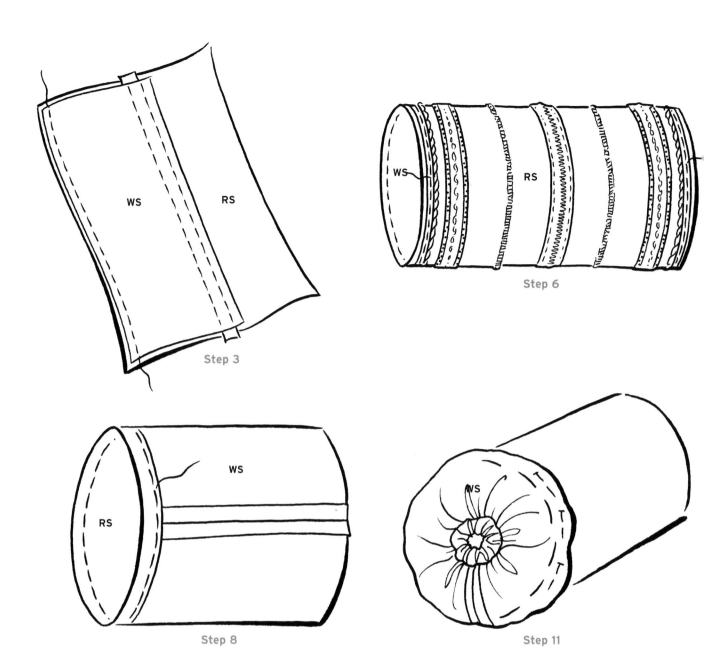

WS

RS

Step 3

WS

RS

Step 6

RS

WS

Step 8

WS

T

T

T

Step 11

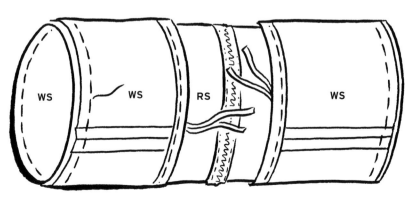

WS

WS

RS

WS

Step 12

## MATERIALS

- ⅞ yard (0.8 m) fabric for pillow body and ends
- ⅞ yard (0.8 m) fabric for contrasting center
- ⅞ yard (0.8 m) of 1" (2.5 cm) -wide grosgrain
- 1¾ yards (1.6 m) of 1¼" (3.2 cm)-wide decorative ribbon
- 2⅝ yards (2.4 m) wide gimp trim
- 1¾ yards (1.6 m) narrow gimp trim
- 1¾ yards (1.6 m) twisted decorative trim with flange
- 2 yards (1.8 m) ¼" (0.6 cm) -wide satin ribbon
- 8½" X 17" (21.6 X 43.2 cm) pillow form
- Marking pen
- Safety pin or bodkin

## PROJECT TECHNIQUES

- Edgestitch (page 141)
- Slipstitch (page 141)
- Topstitch (page 141)
- Attaching Twisted Trim (page 147)
- Joining Twisted Trim (page 147)

## Finished Size

8½" X 17" (21.6 X 43.2 cm)

## Preparation

Cut two pieces of pillow fabric 6" X 28" (15.2 X 71.1 cm) for pillow sections.

Cut two pieces of pillow fabric 6" X 28" (15.2 X 71.1 cm) for pillow ends.

Cut one piece of contrasting fabric 8" X 28" (20.3 X 71.1 cm) for pillow center.

Sew a strip of wide gimp trim to the center of the grosgrain ribbon.

Sew a strip of wide gimp trim to the center of the 1¼" (3.2 cm) -wide decorative ribbon.

Cut the grosgrain into two equal lengths.

Cut the decorative ribbon into two equal lengths.

Cut the satin ribbon into two equal lengths.

## Construction

**Step 1** Center the grosgrain on the length of the right side of the contrasting pillow center. Edgestitch both edges of the ribbon.

**Step 2** Pin a piece of decorative ribbon to the length of the right side of each pillow section, placing the ribbon ¾" (1.9 cm) from the opposite long edges of each section. Edgestitch both sides of each ribbon strip.

**Step 3** With right sides together, sew each pillow section to the contrasting center, aligning the untrimmed edges. Press the seam allowances open.

**Step 4** Center a piece of the narrow gimp trim over the right side of each seam and stitch them in place.

**Step 5** With right sides together, align the two short edges of the pillow body. Stitch a seam to form a tube. Press the seam allowances open.

**Step 6** Sew the decorative twisted cord to each end of the tube.

**Step 7** With right sides together, sew the short edges of a pillow end together, leaving a small opening (for the ends of a drawstring) ½" (1.2 cm) from one end of the seam.

**Step 8** Press the loose raw edge with the small opening 1½" (1.2 cm) to the wrong side. Topstitch to form a casing for a drawstring.

**Step 9** Repeat steps 7 and 8 at the opposite short edge of the pillow body with the remaining end.

**Step 10** Using a safety pin or a bodkin, feed a piece of the satin ribbon through the casing. Draw up the fabric as tightly as possible and tie the ribbon ends to secure.

**Step 11** Turn the end wrong side out and fan the fabric end into a ring. Center the pillow end over the end of the bolster form and smooth the fabric onto the sides. Temporarily pin the raw edges in place. Mark the ends (seamlines) of the bolster form on the pillow ends. Repeat to mark the opposite pillow end.

**Step 12** Remove the pillow ends from the form, release the drawstring ties and flatten the fabric. Staystitch along each marked line. Add a seam allowance beyond the staystitched line on each pillow end and cut off the excess fabric.

**Step 13** With right sides together, slip the end sections over the pillow tube. Using a zipper foot, sew the ends to the pillow along the staystitching line.

**Step 14** Insert the form into the tube and draw up the fabric at each end. Tie the drawstrings to secure the form inside. Trim the ends to an appropriate length. Cut two small pieces of fabric, insert one through the opening at each end. Tack it to the casing if needed.

# Ruched Pillow

WHEN ADDED TO EACH SIDE, the ruched–or shirred–edges give this pillow a vintage look, something precious and passed down. A small bit of exquisite fabric, such as silk brocade, and a coordinating solid-color silk can easily transform a simple pillow into a keepsake.

## MATERIALS

- ½ yard (0.5 m) fabric for pillow front
- ½ yard (0.5 m) coordinating solid-color fabric for the ruching and the pillow back
- Perle cotton thread or heavy thread
- 18" (45.7 cm) square down-and-feather pillow form

## PROJECT TECHNIQUES

- Slipstitch (page 141)

## Finished Size

18" X 18" (45.7 X 45.7 cm)

## Preparation

Cut one piece of fabric 13" X 18" (33 X 45.7 cm) for the front panel.

Cut two pieces of coordinating fabric 4"X 36" (10 X 91.4 cm) for the ruched trim.

Cut one piece of coordinating fabric 18½" X 18½" (46.3 X 46.3 cm) for the pillow back.

## Construction

**Step 1** Along both long edges of a ruching strip of fabric, lay a piece of perle cotton thread on each seamline. Machine zigzag stitch over the perle cotton for the length of the strip. Repeat for the second strip of fabric.

**Step 2** Anchor one end of each perle cotton thread length to the fabric with a straight pin. Hold the other end of each strand of perle cotton and pull it, to gather the fabric to a length of 18" (45.7 cm). Repeat for the second strip of fabric.

**Step 3** With right sides together and using ½" (1.2 cm) seam allowances, sew one long edge of each strip to opposite sides of the center panel. Lightly press the seam allowances toward the strips. Open and lightly press the ruched strips away from the center panel.

**Step 4** With right sides together and using ½" (1.2 cm) seam allowances, sew the pillow back to the front, leaving an opening along one edge for turning.

**Step 5** Turn the pillow cover right-side-out. Insert the form and slip-stitch the opening closed.

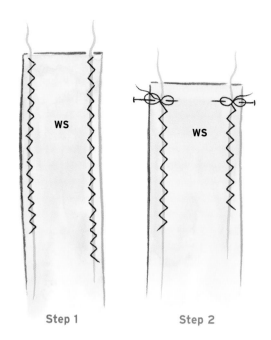

Step 1                    Step 2

Step 3

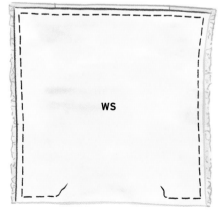

Step 4

## Tip

TO SECURELY ANCHOR THE THREAD AT ONE END, USE A LARGE PIN AS A TOGGLE, AND WRAP THE THREAD AROUND IT.

# Tassel Table Runner

A CONTRASTING BORDER frames this luxurious jacquard table runner. The corners look complicated, but the mitering techniques are actually quite simple. A tassel weights each end just right.

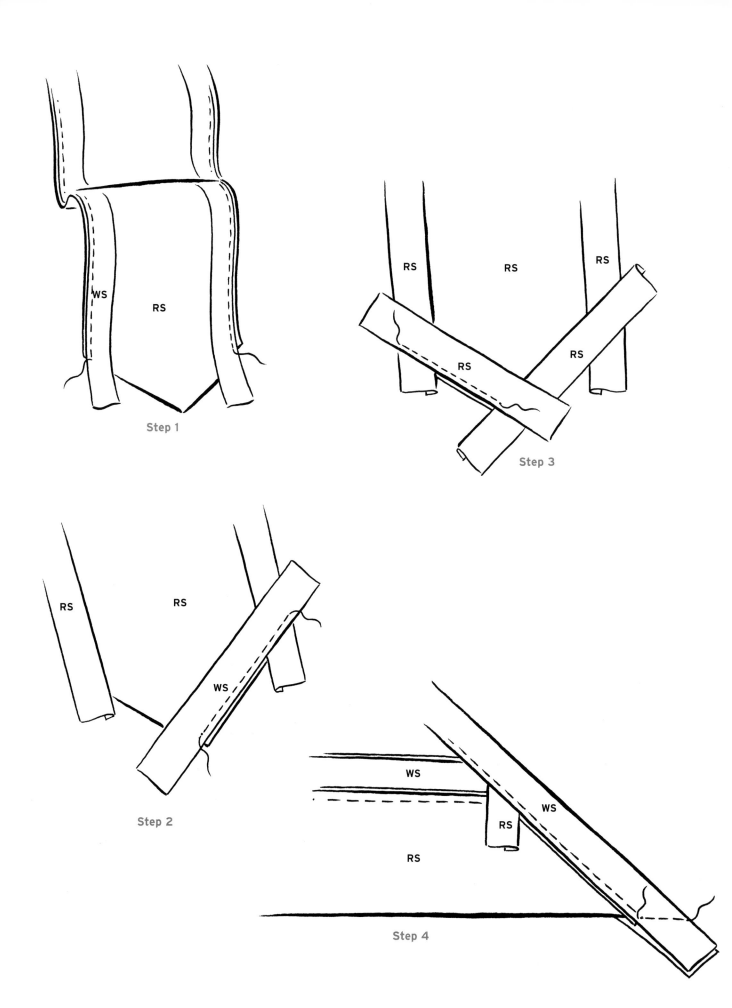

Step 1

Step 3

Step 2

Step 4

## MATERIALS

- *Fabric for the runner*
- *Contrasting fabric for the border*
- *Lining fabric*
- *2 tassels*
- *L-square*
- *Marking pencil*
- *Pattern paper*

## PROJECT TECHNIQUES

- *Slipstitch (page 141)*
- *Topstitch (page 141)*

## Preparation

Decide the finished width and length of the runner, adding length as desired for the amount the runner will hang over the end of the table.

Using pattern paper, draw the length and width of the runner, using an L-square to cut the 90 degree (right) angle at each end. Subtract 2" (5.1 cm) from each edge and then add ½" (1.2 cm) seam allowances to all the edges.

Cut two strips of contrasting fabric 3" (7.6 cm)-wide X the length of the runner plus 6" (15.2 cm) for the side border.

Cut four strips of contrasting fabric 3" (7.6 cm)-wide X the length of each angled side plus 9" (22.9 cm) for the end borders.

Reserve the lining fabric to cut later.

## Construction

**Step 1** With right sides together and using ½" (1.2 cm) seam allowances, sew the contrasting strips to each long edge of the runner. Allow 3" (7.6 cm) to extend past each end. Press the seam allowances toward the border.

**Step 2** With the attached border pressed away from the runner, place the right side of one short contrasting strip over the attached border and extending 3" (7.6 cm) beyond the center point. Using ½" (1.2 cm) seam allowances, sew the border to the runner, stitching through the attached border to the corner, and stopping the stitching ½" (1.2 cm) from the bottom raw edge. Press the border and seam allowances away from the runner.

**Step 3** Repeat step 2 for the adjacent border strip, ending the stitching at the same corner point. Sew across the side border but don't sew on to the border at the point.

**Step 4** With right sides together, fold the runner in half lengthwise through the corner point. Using the foldline as a guide, draw a line from the foldline through the corner point and extending through the border. Stitch on this line from the corner point through the border. Press the seam allowances open. Trim all the excess border ends.

**Step 5** Press the border and seam allowance away from the runner.

**Step 6** Pin a tassel to the corner point of each end of the runner, placing the tassel portion toward the runner and the tassel's top loop toward the outside edge.

**Step 7** Lay the runner with right sides together on the lining fabric. Cut the lining the exact size of the runner.

**Step 8** Keeping the right sides together, sew all sides together making sure to only catch the tassel's top loop and leaving an opening for turning. Trim the seam allowances and corners. Turn to the outside and slipstitch the opening closed.

**Step 9** Press the edges and topstitch ¼" (0.6 cm) from the edges of the border.

# Block-Pieced Throw

LIKE A QUAINT AND COMFY heirloom, this pieced throw adds charm and character to a sofa or chair. Mix seven fabrics in varying textures and patterns and piece them together in an orderly, eclectic arrangement.

LIKE A QUAINT AND COMFY heirloom, this pieced throw adds charm and character to a sofa or chair. Mix seven fabrics in varying textures and patterns and piece them together in an orderly, eclectic arrangement.

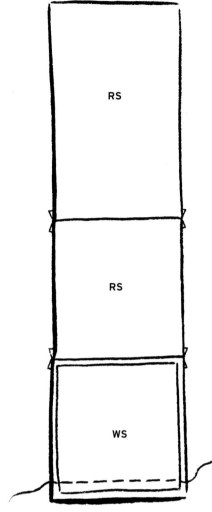

Step 3

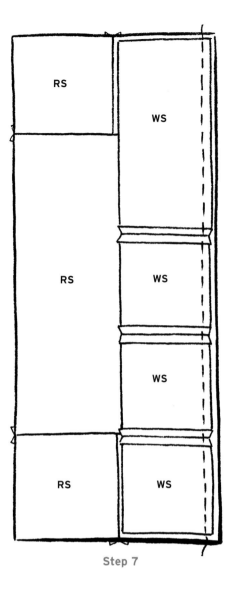

Step 7

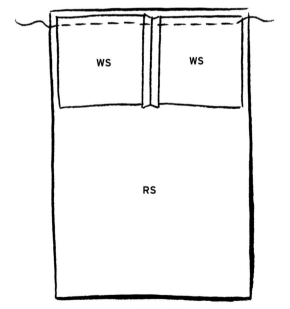

Step 4

### FABRIC BLOCK ASSEMBLY GUIDE
Two blocks shown

### KEY
NUMBER = Recommended fabric

CAPITAL LETTER = Recommended template

-------------------- = Seam joining two pieces cut from the same fabric

ONE FINISHED BLOCK MEASURES 12"X 15" (30.5 X 38.1 CM). IT USES ALL OF THE SEVEN FABRICS, CUT TO SIZE AS FOLLOWS:
FABRIC #1: ONE PIECE SIZE A.
FABRIC #2: TWO PIECES SIZE C.
FABRIC #3: ONE PIECE SIZE C AND ONE PIECE SIZE B.
FABRIC #4: TWO PIECES SIZE C.
FABRIC #5: FOUR PIECES SIZE C.
FABRIC #6: ONE PIECE SIZE B.
FABRIC #7: ONE PIECE SIZE C.

## MATERIALS

- *7 coordinating fabrics for the top*
- *1½" yards (1.4 m) 52" (132 cm)-wide lining fabric*
- *4 tassels*
- *Tag board*

## PROJECT TECHNIQUES

- *Slipstitch (page 141)*

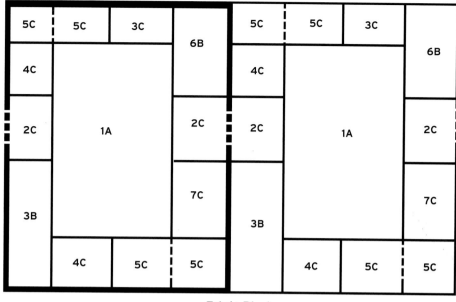

**Fabric Block**

## Finished Size

45" X 48" (114.3 X 121.9 cm)

## Preparation

Make tag board templates in the following shapes:
Size A: 6½" X 9½" (16.5 X 24.1 cm)
Size B: 3½" X 6½" (8.9 X 16.5 cm)
Size C: 3½" X 3½" (8.9 X 8.9 cm)

All the templates include ¼" (0.6 cm) seam allowances.

Cut the following fabrics, using the tag board templates as patterns, to make shapes for 12 blocks:
Cut 12 pieces of fabric #1 to size A.
Cut 24 pieces of fabric #2 to size C.
Cut 12 pieces of fabric #3 to size C.
Cut 12 pieces of fabric #3 to size B.
Cut 24 pieces of fabric #4 to size C.
Cut 48 pieces of fabric #5 to size C.
Cut 12 piece of fabric #6 to size B.
Cut 12 pieces of fabric #7 to size C.
Reserve the lining to cut later.

## Construction

**Step 1** Starting at the top center of one block, sew piece 5C to piece 3C with right sides together. Press the seam allowances open.

**Step 2** At the bottom center of the block, sew piece 4C to piece 5C with right sides together. Press the seam allowances open.

**Step 3** For the right side of the block and starting at the top, sew pieces 6B, 2C, 7C, and 5C together in that order. Press the seam allowances open.

**Step 4** For the left side of the block and starting at the top, sew pieces 5C, 4C, 2C, and 3B together in that order. Press the seam allowances open.

**Step 5** With right sides together, sew the top sequence (5C and 3C) to the top of piece 1A. Press the seam allowances open.

**Step 6** With right sides together, sew the bottom sequence (4C and 5C) to the bottom of piece 1A. Press the seam allowances open.

**Step 7** Sew the right side sequence (6B, 2C, 7C, and 5C) to the right side of joined pieces 3C, 1A, and 5C. Press the seam allowances open.

**Step 8** Sew the left side sequence (5C, 4C, 2C, and 3B) to joined pieces 5C, 1A, and 4C. Press the seam allowances open.

**Step 9** Repeat steps 1 through 8 to make eleven more blocks.

**Step 10** With right sides together, sew four blocks together at the long sides to make a row. Repeat to make two more rows. Sew the rows together to make a complete quilt top.

**Step 11** Lay the right side of the quilt top on the right side of the lining fabric and cut the lining to fit the quilt top.

**Step 12** Pin one tassel to the right side of each corner, placing the tassel portion toward the center of the quilt and the tassel loop toward the outside edge (in the seam allowance).

**Step 13** With right sides together, sew the quilt top to the lining, leaving an opening for turning. Turn the throw to the outside and slipstitch the opening closed.

# Button-Quilted **Throw**

THIS UNUSUAL THROW becomes part of the chaise lounge, adding dimension and softness, as if it were a permanent feature. Bold drapery tiebacks or tassels adorn the corners and define the scale of the piece.

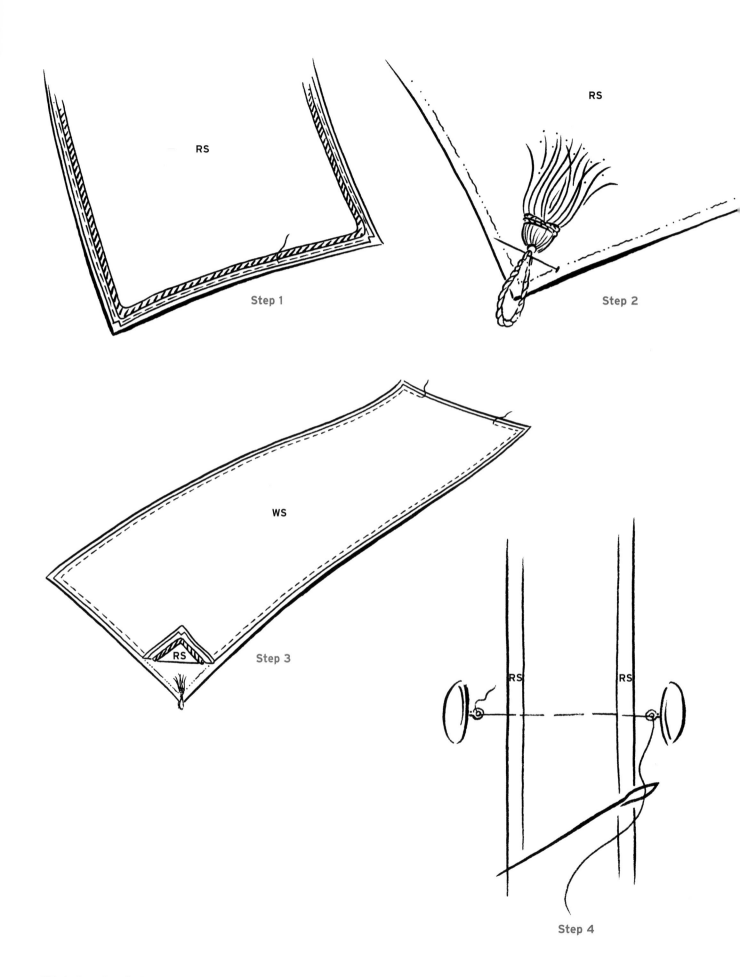

RS

RS

**Step 1**

**Step 2**

WS

RS

**Step 3**

RS

RS

**Step 4**

## MATERIALS

- Fabric
- Decorative trim with flange
- Thick polyester batting
- 4 large tassels
- Cordonnet or heavy thread
- ¾" (1.9 cm) buttons with shanks
- Temporary spray adhesive
- Upholstery needle

## PROJECT TECHNIQUES

- Attaching Back-to-Back Buttons (page 140)
- Slipstitch (page 141)
- Attaching Twisted Cording (page 147)
- Joining Twisted Cording (page 147)

## Preparation

Cut two pieces of fabric the width and length of the throw plus ½" (1.2 cm) seam allowances on all four sides for the throw front and back.

Cut two layers of batting the same size as the throw pieces. Fuse the layers together using temporary spray adhesive.

## Construction

**Step 1** Using the instructions for Attaching Twisted Cording and Joining Twisted Cording on page 147, sew the decorative twisted trim to the right side of the throw front.

**Step 2** Using the temporary spray adhesive, adhere the batting layers to the wrong side of the throw back.

**Step 3** Place a single tassel on the right side of each corner of the batted throw back piece. Pin each tassel so that fringe is toward the throw and the upper ends are toward the outer edge. Make sure the loop at the very top is in the seam allowance.

**Step 4** With right sides together, sew the front and back of the throw together, leaving an opening for turning.

**Step 5** Turn the throw to the outside and slipstitch the opening closed.

**Step 6** Mark button placements at regular intervals. Attach back-to-back buttons.

## Tip

IF THE TASSEL HEAD IS SO BULKY THAT IT IS DIFFICULT TO SEW AROUND THE CORNERS, SWITCH TO A ZIPPER PRESSER FOOT ON THE SEWING MACHINE.

# CHAPTER THREE

# Your Tool Box

ASIDE FROM A RELIABLE SEWING MACHINE and a well-lit work space, the right notions and tools are essential for performing many special sewing tasks. In addition, having the right items in your tool box will save time and add a professional appearance to a finished project. This chapter recommends items that will be helpful to have on hand when making any of the projects in this book.

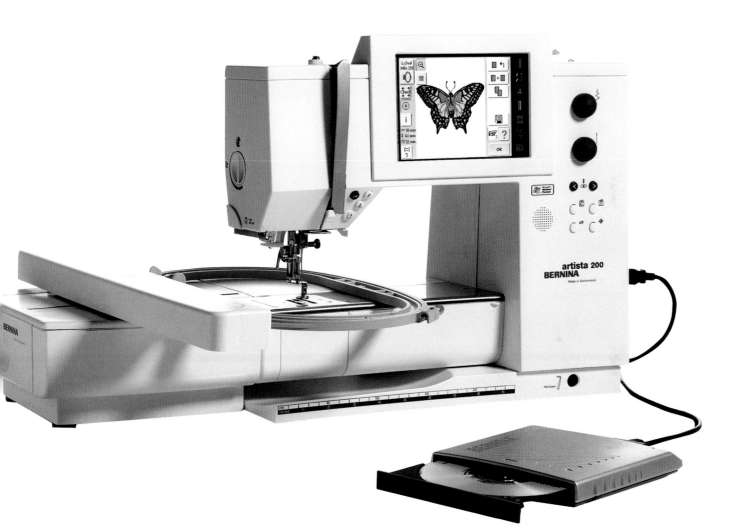

A GOOD, RELIABLE SEWING MACHINE IS THE FOUNDATION FOR ACHIEVING THE MOST PROFESSIONAL RESULTS IN ANY PROJECT. THE MORE FEATURES THAT ARE AVAILABLE ON YOUR MACHINE, THE MORE OPTIONS YOU HAVE FOR CUSTOMIZING YOUR WORK.

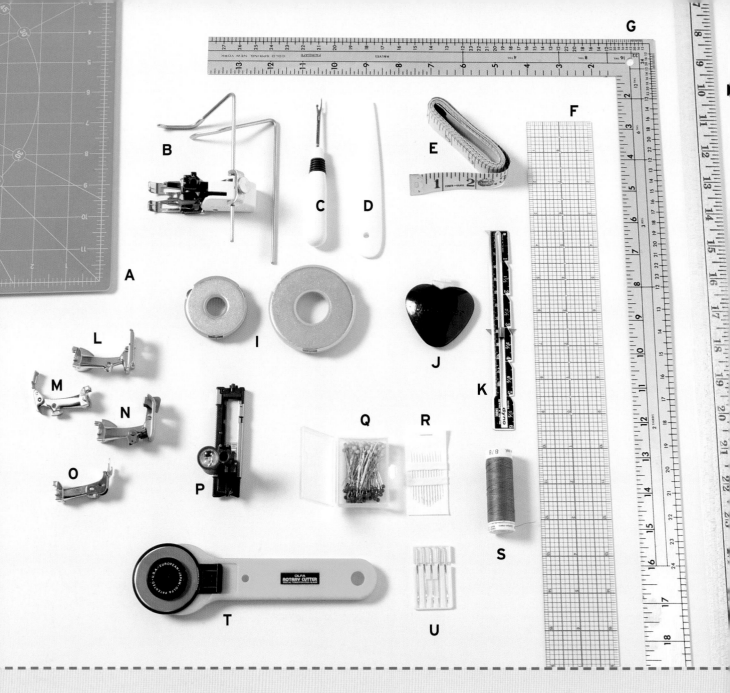

**A** Cutting Mat

**B** Walking Foot

**C** Seam Ripper

**D** Point Turner

**E** Tape Measure

**F** Grid Ruler

**G** L-Square

**H** Yardstick

**I** Weights

**J** Chalk Marker

**K** Seam Gauge

**L** Piping Foot

**M** Zipper Foot

**N** Edgestitch Foot

**O** Button Foot

**P** Button Hole
Presser Foot

**Q** Pins

**R** Hand-Sewing
Needles

**S** Thread

**T** Rotary Cutter

**U** Sewing Machine
Needles

# CUTTING AND SEWING

### Hand-Sewing Needles

A sharp point and an eye that is easily threaded are the two ingredients for fine hand sewing needles. Find the one that feels good in your hand and pierces the fabric cleanly. Crewel embroidery needles in sizes 7–10 work best. Also add a straight upholstery needle to the tool kit.

### Pinking Shears

Heavy shears with a serrated blade (a sharp zigzag) are useful for trimming and finishing raw edges that ravel easily.

### Scissors and Shears

Shears have bent handles that allow them to lie flat and glide on the cutting surface. Scissors have straight rather than angled handles. Long 8" (20.3 cm) shears are best for cutting fabric and smaller 5" (12.7 cm) scissors are good for trimming and clipping.

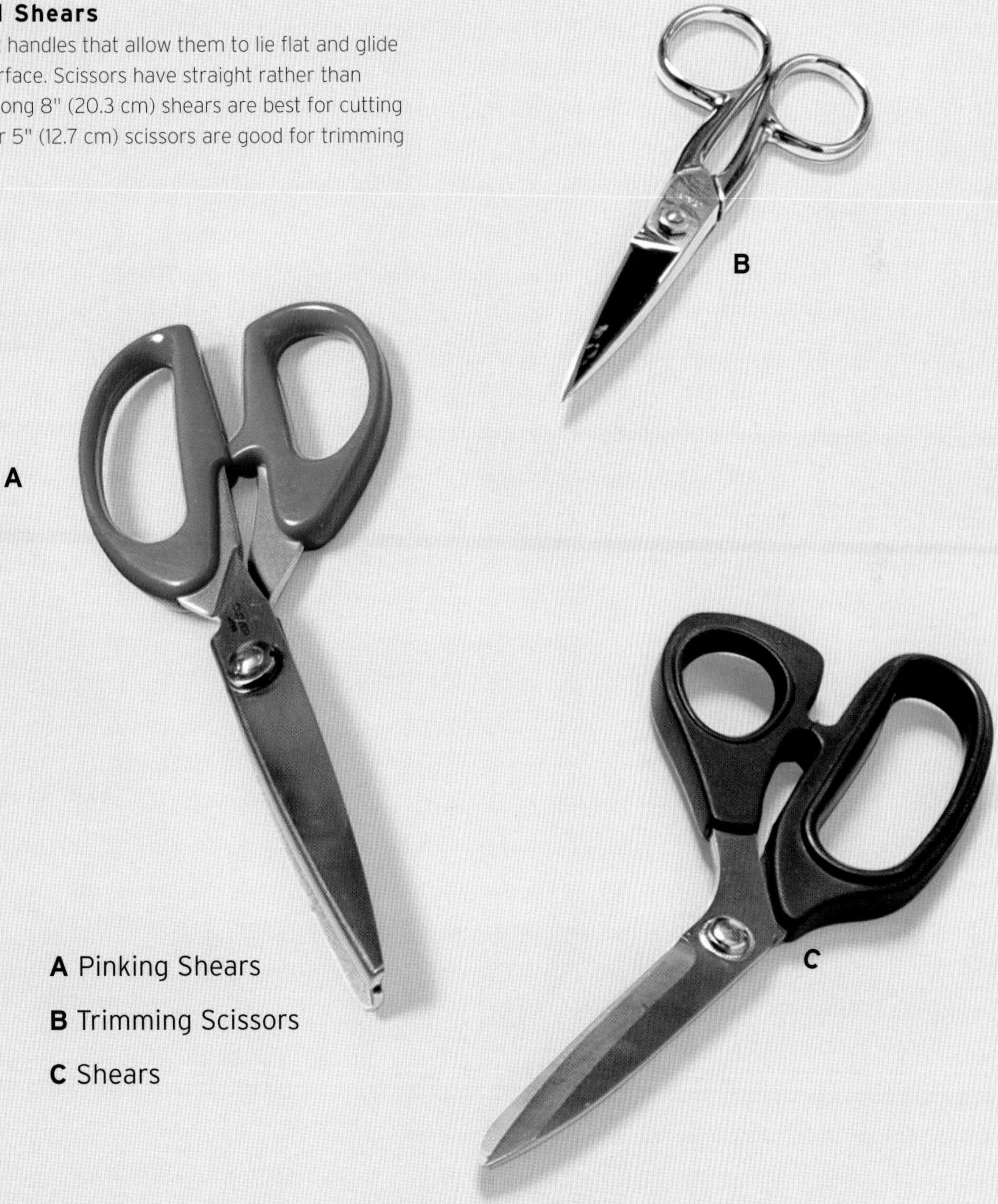

**B**

**A**

**A** Pinking Shears

**B** Trimming Scissors

**C** Shears

**C**

# TOOLS AND NOTIONS

## Pins

There are two pin types to have on hand. Large stainless steel dressmaker pins with large plastic heads are useful when pinning upholstery weight fabrics. Smaller glass-head pins with fine points are best for sheer and lightweight fabrics. Change your pin supply often to avoid bent and dull points.

## Point Turner

This small, soft-edged plastic hand tool is about 5" (12.7 cm) long, with one end that tapers to a point. It helps push the fabric to an edge or fine-tune a corner point.

## Rotary Cutter and Cutting Mat

A rotary cutter is a handy tool that has a circular blade attached to a plastic handle. It operates like a pizza cutter. The cut line is very precise. A cutting mat is required when using a rotary cutter to keep from dulling the blade and to prevent the cutter from marring your work surface. This type of mat is made of a special, soft plastic that is self-healing. Buy the largest mat you can to avoid moving it often when cutting out large projects.

## Seam Ripper

This small hand tool has a sharp point and a tiny cutting edge to aid in removing stitches without harming the fabric. Slip the point under a single stitch and slide the blade to cut the thread.

## Serger

This time-saving machine stitches, trims, and overcasts a seam, all in one step. Used for both finishing, construction, and embellishing, the results are professional, but easy to achieve.

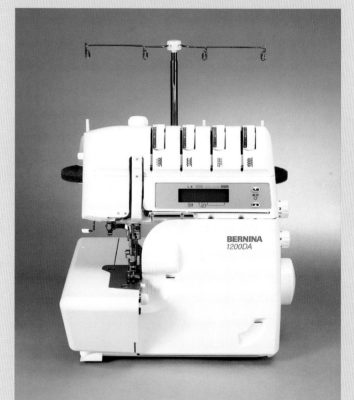

## Sewing Machine Feet
There are a few feet that are used routinely when sewing home decorating projects.

### Button Foot
This foot enables you to sew on buttons with a secure zigzag stitch. The feed dogs need to be dropped to prevent the fabric from moving while sewing.

### Buttonhole Foot
Designed to be used with the automatic settings on the sewing machine, this foot is grooved on the bottom of the foot to glide over and feed the stitches as the buttonhole is sewn.

### Edgestitch Foot
The upright guide blade of this foot rides along the edge of a fold, edge or seamline, acting as a guide for precise straight stitching.

### Piping Foot
This is a presser foot with a cut-out groove on the underside that rides over cording and other trims, guiding the stitching evenly next to the trim. The needle can be positioned to the left or the right of the piping and shifted so the stitches are close to it.

### Walking Foot
This presser foot is an extra accessory to a sewing machine. It allows two pieces of fabric to feed through the sewing machine at the same rate and prevents creeping. It is especially useful when matching plaids or patterns or quilting layers of batting to a fabric.

### Zipper Foot
Depending on the brand of sewing machine, either the needle position moves or the foot moves to position the needle to one side of the foot. This allows you to sew very close to an element that has three-dimensional form, such as a zipper or piping.

## Sewing Machine Needles
Universal needles are appropriate for most sewing projects. Change the needle before beginning a new project and determine the needle size for the weight of the fabric—the finer the fabric, the smaller the needle size. A size 80/12 is a standard size for most projects.

## Thread
Using a good quality thread will improve your production time and the final look of the project. All-purpose, 100 percent cotton is the most universal thread for most projects, although polyester thread is common, too. If puckering becomes a problem, then polyester thread may be the culprit. In several projects, cordonnet thread is recommended for hand sewing. This is a sturdy thread. Choose a weight that is suitable for the fabric and the use. In all cases, use a thread that color-matches the project material for seaming. A contrasting color may be suitable for decorative edgestitching and topstitching. Buy a shade that is slightly darker than the fabric.

## Weights
Weights come in many forms, such as flat discs or small filled domes, but any type is useful for holding pattern pieces in place while cutting fabric.

## MEASURING AND MARKING

### Chalk

Use chalk to make temporary marks on the surface of a fabric. In block or pencil form, it lays down a precise, fine line that stays in place long enough to sew but brushes away easily when no longer needed. White is the best color to use.

### L-Square and T-Square

Squares are useful for measuring 45- and 90-degree angles and for finding and marking lengthwise, crosswise, and bias grains on fabric.

### Ruler

A yardstick (or a 36" [91.4 cm] -long metal ruler) is handy when cutting large pieces of fabric for window coverings, slipcovers, and bed covers. An 18" (45.7 cm -long clear grid ruler works well for smaller projects such as pillows and small accessories. In addition to being useful measuring tools, good rulers also aid in cutting straight, accurate edges.

### Seam Gauge

This small 6" (15.2 cm)-long metal ruler has a sliding marker that is helpful for marking topstitching lines and smaller measurements during construction.

### Tape Measure

A flexible 60" (152.4 cm) cloth or fiberglass tape measure is essential for taking measurement of all kinds. Look for one that starts one at both ends, on opposite sides of the tape.

## PRESSING

### Iron

A good quality steam iron is essential when sewing. Press consistently throughout the construction process, but do not overpress: holding the iron in place too long will leave scorch marks.

### Point Presser

This wooden piece of equipment sits on the ironing board and has a narrow rail on top of a larger wood base (clapper). It helps press hard-to-reach place such as seams, curves and corners.

### Sleeve Board

Use this double-sided, small ironing board when pressing hard-to-reach places, such as fabric tubes, pillows, or small trimmed areas.

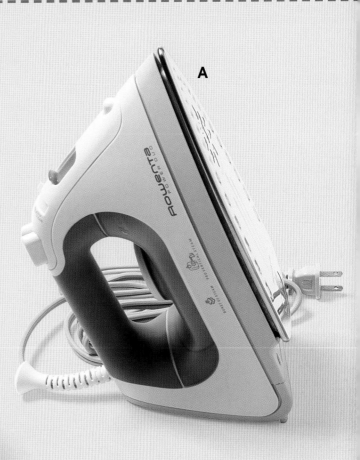

**A** Iron

**B** Point Presser

**C** Sleeve Board

CHAPTER FOUR

# Basic Techniques

# ATTACHING BUTTONS

### Attaching Sew-Through Buttons

To attach a sew-through button, thread a needle and knot the end. Make one stitch on the right side of the fabric at the spot where the button will be attached. Hold the button in place and insert the needle up through one hole in the button. Working on the right side of the fabric, make several stitches through the holes, leaving some slack in the stitches. At the last stitch, bring the needle between the fabric and the bottom of the button. Wrap the thread around the stitches several times to form a shank. Secure the thread on the right side with several small stitches close to the shank.

A button with a metal shank is sewn on in the same manner, passing the needle several times through the fabric and the eye of the shank, then pulling the thread taut, before tying it.

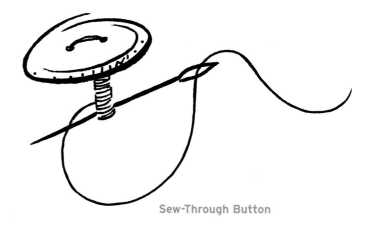

Sew-Through Button

### Attaching Back-to-Back Buttons

Back-to-back buttons are attractive option and act like tufting for a pillow.

Knot one end of a heavy thread, such as cordonnet, to the shank of one covered button and thread the other end of an upholstery needle.

Insert the needle through the center of the pillow. Remove the needle and pull the thread taut. Tie the loose end of the cordonnet thread, to the second button. Trim the excess thread.

### Buttonholes

The size of a buttonhole should always be determined by the size of the button. Minimum buttonhole length should equal the diameter of the button plus the thickness of the button plus an additional 1/8" (0.3 cm) to allow for the shank and a slight size reduction due to the fabric thickness. Machine-made buttonholes should be made through at least two layers of fabric. Follow the instructions included in your sewing machine manual for specific settings and always make a test buttonhole on a scrap of fabric before cutting a buttonhole into your project.

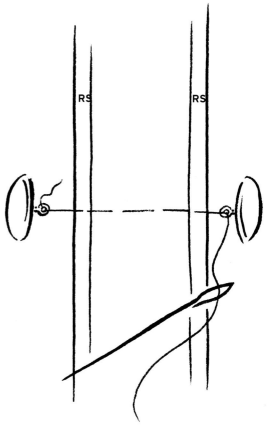

Back-To Back Button

# COMMON SEWING TECHNIQUES

## Baste

Basting is a temporary stitch used to hold pieces of fabric together. Basting improves the accuracy of aligning seams and preventing fabrics from creeping. Basting is an elongated stitch that's sewn by hand or machine and is generally done alongside the seamline for easy removal.

## Double-Fold Hem

A fabric is folded twice to the wrong side, to completely encase the raw edge. In the project instructions, the finished width of the double-fold hem is specified. *In other words, if the project calls for a $\frac{1}{2}$" (1.2 cm)-wide double-fold hem, the hem allowance needs to be 1" (2.5 cm)-wide. Proceed to make the hem in the following manner:

Fold half the width of the hem allowance to the wrong side. Press it in place.

Fold the remaining hem allowance to the wrong side, encasing the previous fold. Press the folded hem allowance and then topstitch near the inner folded edge.

## Edgestitch

Edgestitching is almost like topstitching, except the machine stitching is done through all the fabric layers, as close to a fold or edge as possible. Use an edgestitch presser foot to improve the accuracy of the stitching.

## Finish

A seam finish prevents a seam allowance from raveling, adds durability, and contributes to the overall neatness of the project. Optional finishes include trimming with pinking shears, overlocking the edge on a serger, machine zigzagging, turning the edge to the wrong side (turned and stitched) and stitching or binding an edge with a non-bulky fabric (Hong Kong finish).

## Slipstitch

The slipstitch is an almost invisible hand stitch used for hems, closing pillow edges, and attaching trims and linings. Working from the right to the left, insert the needle into the folded edge of the upper layer, slide it inside the fold, bring it out about $\frac{1}{4}$" (0.6 cm) from the insertion point, then slide the needle under a single thread of the lower layer. Repeat.

## Staystitch

This machine stitch reinforces a seamline before attaching one piece of fabric to another. Sewn through one layer of fabric, it is used so that the seam allowances can be clipped and spread without tearing beyond the seamline.

## Stitch-in-the-Ditch

This is an invisible method of holding layers of fabric together. The machine stitch is centered in the "well" of the seam, where the two pieces of fabric are joined.

## Topstitch

Both decorative and functional, topstitching is made next to an edge or near a seam through one or more layers of fabric on the top side of the project.

*ALL PROJECTS IN THIS BOOK ARE SEWN USING $\frac{1}{2}$" (1.2 CM) SEAM ALLOWANCES UNLESS OTHERWISE NOTED.

# FABRIC TIES

This process creates a clean, crisp tie that can be narrow or wide. It is not necessary to turn a tube to the outside after seaming.

Determine the desired finished width of the tie. Multiply this number by four. Cut the fabric to the width X the desired length plus 1" (2.5 cm) for seam allowances.

Fold one short end to the wrong side 1/2" (1.2 cm). Fold the tie in half lengthwise and press along the folded edge. Unfold and press each long raw edge to the center foldline.

Again fold the tie in half lengthwise. Edgestitch the three folded edges.

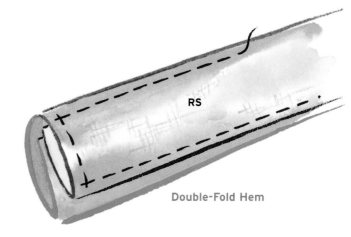

**Double-Fold Hem**

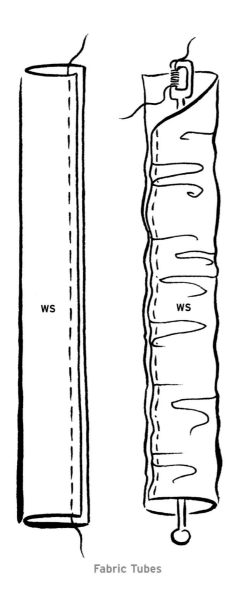

**Fabric Tubes**

# FABRIC TUBES

A ball-point bodkin is an essential tool when turning fabric tubes. Fold a fabric strip in half lengthwise with right sides together. Stitch along the seam line to form a tube and trim the seam to ⅛" (0.3 cm).

Insert the ball-point bodkin into the tube. Hand stitch through the eye of the bodkin several times securing the top to the top of the tube. Push the bodkin through the center of the tube, gradually exposing the right side of the fabric to the outside.

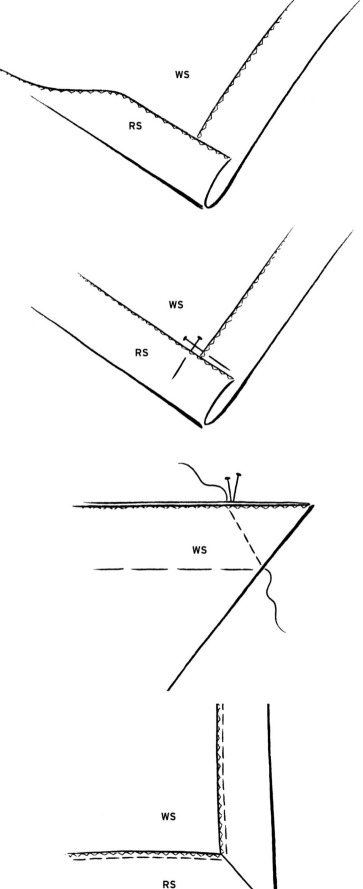

## MITERED HEMS

A miter is a diagonal seam at a corner. It gives the corner a clean and finished look on the inside and eliminates fabric bulk at the same time.

Finish the raw edge. Turn the hem allowances at adjacent corners to the wrong side and press.

On adjacent sides of a corner where the two hems intersect, place pins perpendicularly through the hem only.

Unfold the hem. With right sides together, align the finished edges to form a diagonal fold, matching the pins. Draw a line between the point where the two hem creases and the pins intersect, then stitch.

Trim the excess corner fabric to ¼" (0.6 cm). Press the seam allowances open over a point presser and turn the corner to the inside and press. Topstitch next to the inside fold.

Mitered Hems

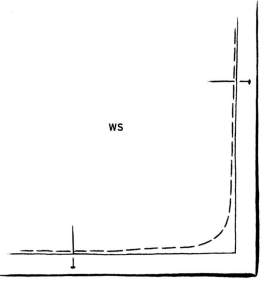

**Knife-Edge Pillows**

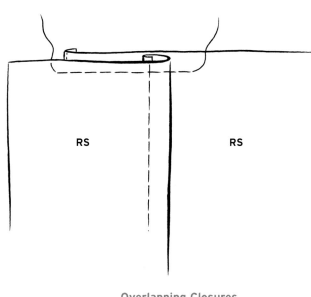

**Overlapping Closures**

# PILLOW BASICS

### Knife-Edge Pillows

Knife-edge pillows have two pieces of fabric that are sewn together with one continuous seam around the outside edges. This technique prevents "dog-eared" corners.

Start by pinning the front and back pillow pieces, with right sides together, around the four sides.

Measure the length of one side and divide this number by 4. Do the same for the remaining sides. Mark a point one-fourth of the side from each corner. Pin-mark this quarter distance from the corner. Do the same for the remaining sides. Mark 1/2" (1.2 cm) seam allowances parallel to all four edges of the pillow pieces. Measure the length of each side and divide into quarters. Mark a point one-fourth of the side from each corner.

Sew the seam, starting to taper inward at the pinmark immediately preceding each corner point. The taper should be a minimum of 1/4" (0.6 cm). The heavier the fabric, the more exaggerated the taper.

 Generally, the excess fabric is not trimmed out of the corners. When the pillow is turned right side out, the seam allowances help fill out the corners and soften the points.

### Overlapping Closures

An overlap is a finished opening on the back of a pillow that allows the easy insertion of a pillow form or its easy removal for cleaning. It can also be a decorative element when planned in advance.

Divide the finished pillow back measurement in half. To one half, add 4" (10 cm) for an underlap. To the other half,

add 1 1/2" (3.8 cm) for an overlap. Add 1/2" (3.8 cm) seam allowances to the remaining edges. Cut these two pieces to construct the back. To the underlap edge, turn 1/2" (1.2 cm) to the wrong side and edgestitch. To the overlap edge, turn the raw edge to the wrong side 1/2" (1.2 cm) and then another 1" (2.5 cm). Stitch close to the inside folded edge.

Lay the wrong side of the overlap half of the pillow back over the underlap side. Baste the two pieces together along the seam allowances of both sides.

### Pillow Forms

Pillow forms are available in two varieties—polyester or down-and-feather filled. Polyester forms are more readily available and less expensive. While soft, they retain their original shape and cannot be manipulated into another shape or size.

Down-and-feather filled forms are available in a number of qualities and the range of prices reflects these differences. These forms are soft and squishy and have a more relaxed look than polyester forms.

When using polyester forms, cut the pillow pieces 1" (2.5 cm) larger than the form to add seam allowances. For example, a 20" (50.8 cm) square polyester pillow form requires cut pieces of 21" (53.3). Pillow pieces for down-and-feather forms are cut the exact size of the form and the seam allowances are considered included. Cut 20" (50.8 cm) square sections when using a 20" (50.8 cm) square down-and-feather form.

# PIPING

Also called welting, or covered cording, piping is a narrow, bias, cord-filled strip of fabric with a seam allowance, also called a flange, which is inserted into a seam for a decorative accent.

Purchase at least ½ yard (0.5 m) of fabric to cut bias strips for pillow projects. One yard (0.9 m) of fabric is enough extra fabric for larger projects.

Cable cord is a tubular filler made in cotton or other blends. It is sold in packages or by the yard in several diameters.

## Cutting Bias Strips

Strips of fabric to cover cable cord for piping should be cut on the true bias.

True bias can be found by folding one selvage edge of a piece of fabric 45 degrees, creating a diagonal fold. Draw lines, usually about 2" (5.1 cm) apart for standard piping, parallel to the fold. Cut along the marked lines. Bias strips have more stretch than fabric strips cut on the straight of grain to enable the fabric to wrap around the cording smoothly and for the finished piping to lie smoothly at curves and corners.

## Joining Bias Strips

To sew continuous strips together, place two strips right sides together with the ends aligned, matching the edges where the seam will be sewn. Press the seam allowances open. Continue sewing strips together in the same manner to make the total length needed.

## Making Covered Piping

To make covered piping, attach a zipper foot or a cording/piping foot (see page 135) onto your sewing machine. Move the needle position toward the piping, if needed.

Center the cable cord on the wrong side of the bias strip. Fold the strip over the cord, aligning the raw edges. Place the covered cord under the presser foot with the cord to the left of the needle and the seam allowance to the right. Stitch close to the cord. Trim the seam allowance to an even ½" (1.2 cm).

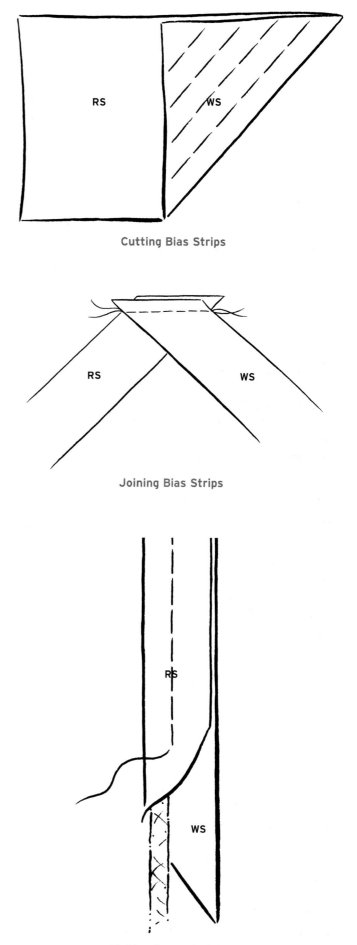

**Cutting Bias Strips**

**Joining Bias Strips**

**Making Covered Piping**

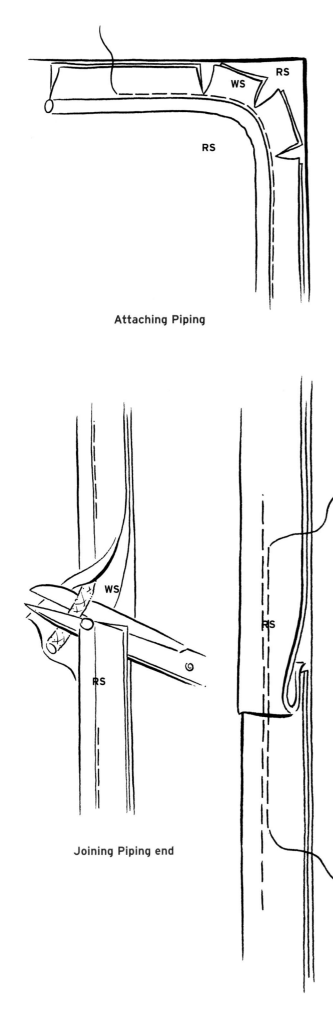

**Attaching Piping**

**Joining Piping end**

## Attaching Piping

To attach covered piping, pin it to one edge of the right side of the fabric front of the main portion of the project, with the piping's seam allowances closest to the raw edges.

Install a zipper or cording presser foot on the sewing machine. Position the piping next to the presser foot and stitch over the previous (piping) stitching. Begin sewing about 1½" (3.8 cm) from the end of the piping.

Using the same principle as sewing a knife-edge pillow (see page 144), taper the placement of the piping to the inside at the corners. About 1" (2.5 cm) from the corner, insert the needle through the fabric layers to hold the work in place. Make three clips through the flange. Continue stitching the rounded corner.

To attach another piece of fabric, such as the pillow back or a boxing strip, place the right sides of the new fabric against the right side of the piped piece. Align the cut edges and pin along the previous line of stitching. Move the needle position closer to the piping and sew right next to the previous stitching.

## Joining Piping Ends

Plan to join the piping in the center of a bottom edge of a pillow, where it will be less visible. Leave both ends of the piping free for about 1½" (3.8 cm), then overlap them and cut the excess from the finishing end about 1½" (3.8 cm) from beyond the starting end. Remove the piping stitching that secures the cord. Expose the cord and cut it so that it butts with the cord at the start of the seam.

Fold the end of the finishing end to the wrong side and place the starting end of the piping on it. Wrap the bias covering over the joint. Position the piping along the seamline and complete the seam.

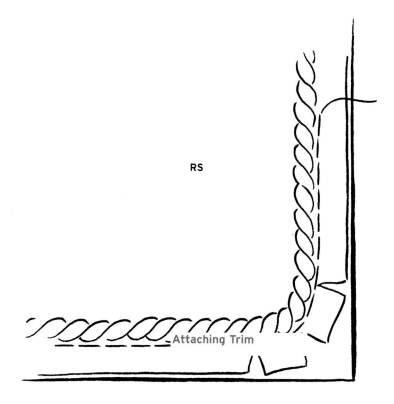

RS

Attaching Trim

# DECORATIVE TRIM

Decorative trim is a purchased trim that may have a twisted cord, tassels, fringe, beads or any number of interesting elements, all of which are attached to a tapelike flange. The flange is sewn into a seam along an edge.

### Attaching Twisted Cording

Sew the trim to the right side of the pillow front in the same manner as attaching covered piping (see page 146). Leave about 3" (7.6 cm) of extra trim at each end and leave about 1 ½" (3.8 cm) of space where the trim is not sewn to the edge.

### Joining Twisted Cording

Separate the flange from the cord. Carefully separate the individual strands of twisted cord and tape each end if the ends tend to fray. Overlap the ends of the loose flange and tape them together with cellophane or masking tape. Place the lefthand tails facing up and the left-hand tails down.

Tape the left-hand tails over the taped flange, twisting the tails back into its original order.

Manipulate the right-hand tails to return the individual strands to their original order, weaving them into the left-hand strands in the correct order. Tape the strands to the flange.

Using a zipper foot or cording foot, stitch through all the taped strands next to the finishing cording. Trim the excess tails; remove and discard the tape.

# YARDAGE CALCULATIONS

It is important to take the time to determine the right amount of fabric to purchase and to cut it out appropriately. A few formulas assist in this process.

## Calculation for Number of Widths

The number of widths is determined by adding the amounts needed for the side hems and the fullness to the finished width of the window treatment or area to be covered.

**Step 1** To the width of the window or the area to be covered, add returns (the distance from the front of the hardware to the wall) and the overlap (the distance that the two sections of fabric overlap in the center of the window).

**Step 2** Multiply the finished width X the desired fullness, usually two and a half times for medium weight fabric and three times for sheer fabrics.

**Step 3** Add the side hem allowances for the total width required.

**Step 4** Divide the total width including side hem allowances by the fabric width to arrive at the total number of fabric widths needed.

If the number of widths determined is not a whole number, round it off. If the fraction is ½ or greater, round off to the next whole number. Round off to the smaller number if the fraction is less than ½.

Most curtains and draperies open at the center and each half is called a panel, no matter how many widths of fabric are included.

## Calculation for Total Yardage

**Step 5** Add the length of the window opening to the distance above and below the opening to arrive at the finished length. Add the distance above the window where a drapery will hang as well as any puddling at the bottom desired. A drapery normally sits ½" (1.2 cm) above the floor or above the sill if an inside mounting or at the bottom of the casing for an outside mount.

**Step 6** To the finished length, add the top allowance and lower hem allowance specified in each project.

**Step 7** Multiply the cut length by the number of widths to get the total fabric length in inches (cm). Divide the result X 36 (0.9 m) to arrive at the number of yards to purchase. Always add a few inches (or centimeters) for ravel and waste allowances.

## Length Addition for Repeats

Fabrics that have printed or woven designs usually require extra yardage so that the pattern can be matched at the seams.

To determine the vertical repeat, measure lengthwise from the same spot on one motif within the repeat to the same spot in the next identical motif.

Follow the directions for step 6 above.

Divide the cut length measurement X the vertical repeat size. Round up to the next whole number if the result contains a fraction to arrive at the number of pattern repeats needed for each cut length.

Multiply that number by the vertical repeat to determine, in inches, the repeat cut length.

Multiply the repeat cut length X the number of fabric widths to get the total length in inches (cm). Divide by 36 (0.9 m) to convert to yards.

## Seam Positions for Fabric Widths

Full widths of fabric should hang at the leading edge (usually the center) of a treatment. Place partial widths on the sides, where they will be less noticeable.

For an unpatterned fabric, join the widths with normal seam allowances. For a patterned fabric, lay the widths with right sides together and selvages aligned. Fold back the selvage edges until the pattern matches exactly. Slightly press the fold.

Unfold the selvage edges, pin the layers and stitch on the fold. After seaming the widths, trim the panel to the total width required.

# Glossary

**Apron** An apron is the vertical portion of a chair slipcover that extends below the seat. A slipcover may end with the apron, or a skirt may be sewn to the bottom of the apron.

**Baste** Basting is a temporary stitch used to hold pieces of fabric together. Basting improves the accuracy of aligning seams and preventing fabrics from creeping. The basting stitch is an elongated stitch sewn by hand or machine and is generally done alongside the seamline for easy removal.

**Boxing** Boxing is the section of fabric connecting two pieces of fabric to create thickness, as in a boxed pillow.

**Corded Piping** Sometimes referred to as welting, corded piping is a fabric-covered filler (cording), that is sewn into a seam as a decorative trim.

**Cordonnet** Cordonnet is a heavy two-ply cotton thread used to attach buttons and cushions.

**Drop** The drop is the amount of fabric that extends over the edge of a table in a tablecloth or drops to the floor from the box springs to make a dustruffle.

**Edgestitch** Edgestitching is a cousin to topstitching except that the machine stitching is done through all layers as close to a fold or edge as possible. An edgestitch presser foot is a handy accessory that improves the accuracy of the stitch.

**Finish** A seam finish prevents a seam allowance from raveling, adds durability and contributes to the overall neatness of the project. Optional finishes include trimming with pinking shears, overlocking the edge on a serger, machine zigzagging, turning the edge to the wrong side (turned and stitched), and stitching or binding an edge with a non-bulky fabric (Hong Kong finish).

**Flat Piping** Piping is a narrow piece of fabric, folded in half lengthwise with the wrong sides together, and inserted into a seam allowing a portion of the fabric to extend beyond the seam for decorative purposes.

**Flange** A flange is a flat woven tape attached to a decorative trim, the flat extension of fabric as part of corded piping, both of which generally are sewn into and hidden in a seam. The flat fabric extension as part of a pillow or pillow sham is also referred to as a flange.

**Heading** This term refers to the portion of a drapery or curtain that forms the decorative top of a treatment, as in pleats, shirring, tabs, or ties.

**Mounting Board** A mounting board is a piece of wood that is cut to the size of the window treatment, covered with self fabric or lining material, to which the treatment is stapled for installation.

**Panel** A panel is one or more sections of fabric that is joined and finished to become one complete panel.

**Piping** Piping is the cording, generally made in cotton, used to fill the inside of a fabric tube. When filled, the decorative trim is called corded piping.

**Puddling** A designer detail called puddling is a dramatic way to end draperies and curtains at the floor. Add from 2" to 12" (5.1 to 30.5 cm) to the length.

**Slipstitch**

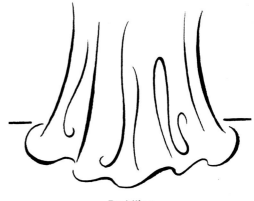
**Puddling**

**Rosette** A rosette is an ornament made of ribbons, threads, or fabric that is gathered or tufted in the shape resembling a rose.

**Slipstitch** The slipstitch is an almost invisible hand stitch used for hems, closing pillow edges, and attaching trims and linings.

**Staystitch** This machine stitch reinforces a seamline before attaching one piece of fabric to another. Sewn through one layer of fabric, it is used so that the seam allowances can be clipped and spread without risk of tearing.

**Topstitch** Both decorative and functional, topstitching is stitched next to an edge or near a seam through one or more layers of fabric on the top side of the project.

**Tufting** Tufting is a method of securing a quilt with a cluster of threads drawn tightly through layers of fabric and batting or adding a decorative tufted design on pillows.

**Stitch-in-the-Ditch** This is an invisible method of holding layers of fabric together. The machine stitch is centered in the "well" of the seam.

**Valance** A valance is a short drapery, shade, or curtain hanging across the top of a window.

**Welting** Welting is a term that is interchangeable with Piping. See Piping page 150.

# Resources

## RETAIL

**A. Baer Company**
505 E. Market Street
Louisville, KY 40202 USA
502.583.5521
www.baerfabrics.com
fabrics, trims, pillow forms

**ABC Carpet & Home**
888 Broadway
New York, NY 10003 USA
212.473.3000
www.ABChome.com
down pillow forms, fabrics, trims

**Bernina Switzerland**
Fritz Gegauf AG
Nahmaschinenfabrik
Seestrasse 161
8266 Steckborn
Switzerland
www.bernina.com
sewing machines

**Bernina of America**
3702 Prairie Lake Court
Aurora, IL 60504 USA
630.978.2500
www.berninausa.com
sewing machines

**Britex**
146 Geary Street
San Francisco, CA 94108 USA
415.392.2910
www.britexfabrics.com
fabrics, trims

**Calico Corners**
800.213.6366
www.calicocorners.com
fabrics, trims, pillow forms, drapery
findings

**Clotilde**
P.O. Box 7500
Big Sandy, TX 75755 USA
800.772.2891
www.clotilde.com
mail order sewing notions

**Designers Guild**
3 Olaf Street
London, WQQ 4BE
United Kingdom
0171.243.7300
www.designersguild.com
fabrics

**Fabric.com**
800-455-2940
www.fabric.com
fabrics

**Gayfeather Fabrics**
1521 Williamson Street
Madison, WI 53701 USA
608.294.7436
www.gayfeatherfabrics.com
fabrics

**Haberman Fabrics**
905 South Main Street
Royal Oak, MI 48067 USA
248.541.0010
www.habermanfabrics.com
down pillow forms, fabrics

**Hancock Fabrics**
www.hancockfabrics.com
fabrics, trims

**Hands of the Hills**
3016 78th Avenue SE
Mercer Island, WA 98040 USA
206.232.8121
www.handsofthehills.com
imported silk fabrics

**Laura Ashley**
Freepost SY1225
P.O. Box 5
Newtown, Powys SY161 LX
United Kingdom
0871.230.2301
www.lauraashley.com
fabrics

**LFN Textiles**
4025 N. Hermitage Avenue
Chicago, IL 60613 USA
773.883.1888
www.lfntextiles.com
specialty ribbon

**Lodi Down & Feather**
973-546-4502
www.lodidownandfeather.com
down pillow forms and bedding

**M&A Linens**
270 W. 39th Street 10th floor
New York, NY 10018 USA
212.869.5078
linen fabrics

**Marimekko Oyi**
Puusepänkatu 4
Finland 00810 Helsinki
358.9.75871
www.marimekko.fi
fabrics

**Mokuba Ribbon**
55 W. 39th Street
New York, NY 10018 USA
212.869.8900
Japanese imported ribbon

**Pat Mahoney**
537 York Street
Lodi, CA 95241 USA
209.369.5410
covered buttons

**Professional Sewing Supplies**
P.O. Box 14272
Seattle, WA 98114 USA
206.324.8823
Japanese sewing notions

**Ruban et Fleur**
7664 Melrose Avenue
Los Angeles, CA 90046 USA
323.653.2227
ribbons, trims

**Sarah's Fabrics**
925 Massachusetts Street
Lawrence, KS 66044 USA
785.842.6198
www.sarahsfabrics.com
fabrics, trims

**Thai Silks**
252 State Street
Los Altos, CA 94022 USA
800.722.7455
www.thaisilks.com
silk fabrics

**Satin Moon Fabrics**
32 Clement Street
San Francisco, CA 94118 USA
415.668.1623
fabrics, tassels, ribbons, pillow
forms

**Sew Natural's Creative Textiles**
453 Cerrillos Road
Santa Fe, NM 87501 USA
505.982.8389
fabrics, drapery findings

**Stone Mountain and Daughter
Fabrics**
2518 Shattuck Avenue
Berkeley, CA 94704 USA
866.473.9386
www.stonemountainfabric.com
fabrics

**Joe's Fabric Warehouse**
102 Orchard Street
New York, NY 10002 USA
212.674.7089
discount decorator fabric

**Vogue Fabrics**
718 Main Street
Evanston, IL 60202 USA
847.864.9600
www.myvoguefabrics.com
fabrics, drapery findings, trims

## TO THE TRADE

**Anna French**
343 Kings Road
London SW3 5GS
United Kingdom
www.annafrench.co.uk
Fabrics

**Brunschwig & Fils**
D&D Building
979 third Avenue,
Suite 1200
New York, NY 10022 USA
www.brunschwig.com
Fabrics, trims

**Donghia Furniture/Textiles Ltd.**
485 Broadway
New York, NY 10013 USA
www.donghia.com
fabrics

**Kravet**
225 Central Avenue South
Bethpage, NY 11714 USA
www.kravet.com
fabrics, trims

**Osborne & Little**
49 Temperley Road
London, 8W12 4EY
United Kingdom
www.osborneandlittle.com
fabrics

**Osborne & Little (USA)**
979 Third Avenue,
Suite 520
New York, NY 10022 USA
www.osborneandlittle.com
fabrics

**JAB**
Stroheim & Romann
155 East 56th Street
New York, NY 10022 USA
www.jab.de
fabrics, decorative drapery rods

**Knoll International Textiles**
105 Wooster Street
New York NY 10012 USA
www.knoll.com
fabrics

**www.ReSources.com**
Direct access to Fabric Product
manufacturers web sites

**Rodolph, Inc.**
P.O. Box 1249
Sonoma, CA 95476 USA
fabrics

**Arthur Sanderson & Sons**
285 Grand Avenue
#3 Patriot Centre
Englewood, NJ 07631 USA
800.894.6185
www.sanderson-uk.com
fabrics and wallcoverings

**Sanderson House**
Oxford Road
Denham UB9 4DX UK
www.sanderson-uk.com
fabrics and wallcoverings

**Zimmer + Rohde**
Zimmersmuhlenweg 14-16
61440 Oberursel/Frankfurt
Germany
www.zimmer-rohde.com
fabrics

# Index

# Acknowledgments

As a dedicated designer who loves the visual stimulation of beautiful interior photographs full of designer details and exquisite colors and fabrics, I was thrilled to work on this book because the photography is such an important feature. Betsy Gammons sent me a collection of the most luscious photographs from which to choose. What an exceptional opportunity to work with her, learn from her professional eye, and to be able to pass along these high-style ideas to the home sewer. Delilah Smittle held all of this together with her organizational skills and her faith that all the pieces would come together.

I thank both of these women for helping me throughout the entire process with a minimum of flap and certainly only the most positive encouragement.

My associates at *e. architects* were kind enough to inquire about the progress of the book from time to time, probably wondering when I would be able to concentrate on my interior design work again.

And of course, my family made sure that I got priority computer time, usually late at night. Husband Craig, and Alex, my daughter, are my real priorities. They are always so understanding, so I thank them for giving me the space and time to do what I love.

# Photographer Credits

Courtesy of Laura Ashley UK/www.lauraashley.com, 104; 117; 120

Tim Beddow/The Interior Archive, 30 (bottom, right)

Courtesy of Bernina of America, Inc./www.bernina.com, 130; 134

Courtesy of Calico Corners/www.calicocorners.com, 15; 25;
     27 (left); 66; 70; 88

Guillaume de Laubier, 39; 42; 62; 124

Tria Giovan, 51; 110

Sam Gray/Leanna Croft, Design, 46

Courtesy of ICI Paints/www.glidden.com, 20; 21; 22

Courtesy of Maine Cottage Furniture/
     www.mainecottage.com, 26

Courtesy of Marimekko Oy/www.marimekko.com, 23 (bottom)

Courtesy of Rod Mickley Interior Design/
     www.rodmickley.com, 72

Allan Penn, 132; 133; 137

Eric Roth/Susan Sargent, Design, 30 (top, left); 31 (middle, left)

Eric Roth, 30 (top, right); 81

Courtesy of Arthur Sanderson & Sons/www.sanderson-uk.com,
     6 (top); 7 (top); 9; 16; 17; 28; 30 (bottom, left); 31
     (top, left); 31 (right); 34; 76; 98; 100; 114; 155

Robin Stubbert, 19

Courtesy of Zimmer + Rohde/www.zimmer-rohde.com,
     6 (bottom); 7 (bottom); 10; 23 (top); 24 (left);
     27 (right); 29; 54; 107

Brian Vanden Brink/Mary Drysdale Associates, 31, (bottom, left)

Brian Vanden Brink/Elliott Elliott Norelius Architecture, 48

Brian Vanden Brink/Coastal Design Consultants, 58; 84

Edina van der Wyck/The Interior Archive, 78

Fritz von der Schulenburg/The Interior Archive, 64; 90; 102

Luke White/The Interior Archive, 93

All illustrations by Liané Roundy

# About the Author

Linda Lee is an ASID Interior Designer and founder of
Linda Lee Design Associates, a corporation consisting of Linda
Lee Interiors and The Sewing Workshop Pattern Collection.
She lectures, writes articles, designs patterns, and has written
several books on designing and sewing home decor and
accessories. She is currently director of Interiors for
*e.architects* in Topeka where she lives and works.